SIMON HOPKINSON COOKS

SIMON HOPKINSON COOKS

EBURY
PRESS

This book is published to accompany the television series entitled
Simon Hopkinson Cooks, first broadcast on More4 in 2013 and produced
by Ricochet Limited, a Shed Media Group Company.

Executive Producer: Simon Knight
Series Producer: Nicola Pointer
Directed by: Jason Lowe

10 9 8 7 6 5 4 3 2 1

Published in 2013 by Ebury Press, an imprint of Ebury Publishing.
A Random House Group Company.

The Random House Group Limited Reg. No. 954009

Addresses for companies within the Random House Group can be found
at www.randomhouse.co.uk

A CIP catalogue record for this book is available from the British Library.

ISBN: 9780091957247

The Random House Group Limited supports the Forest Stewardship
Council® (FSC®), the leading international forest-certification organisation.
Our books carrying the FSC label are printed on FSC®-certified paper. FSC is
the only forest-certification scheme supported by the leading environmental
organisations, including Greenpeace. Our paper procurement policy can be
found at www.randomhouse.co.uk/environment

Commissioning editor: Muna Reyal
Copy-editor: Imogen Fortes
Proofreader: Marion Moisy
Designer: Will Webb
Photography: Jason Lowe
Food stylist: Joe Woodhouse
Production: Helen Everson

Printed and bound in Germany by Firmengruppe APPL, aprinta druck,
Wemding

To buy books by your favourite authors and register for offers,
visit www.randomhouse.co.uk

For Fee

NORTH EAST LINCOLNSHIRE COUNCIL	
01035777	
Bertrams	18/09/2013
641.5	£25.00

Contents

Introduction

Introduction

Cooking is my joy, naturally, and has become my reason for living, but it is my profession, too. However, it constantly amazes me when the public, in general, never quite grasps that a professional cook differs from that of the domestic cook.

To illustrate this curious juxtaposition, it was interesting when an old friend at supper, and to whom, amongst others, I was serving some home-cured gravadlax, spoke up thus – and in the very nicest way: 'Just how do you manage to cut the salmon so thin?'. I was almost speechless, but then quietly muttered 'Um… I guess you might call it expertise?'.

So, there I was in a domestic situation, yet when wielding a whippy sharp knife, a skill of four decades slicing salmon thinly was completely overlooked by my chum (who also happens to be a master of wine). I very nearly parried by suggesting how astonishing that said chum could, without fail, always detect a Bordeaux from a Burgundy in a blind tasting. I didn't – but what if I had?

As a professional cook writing (and making TV series) for home cooks, I also think that what I do should be 'grown-up'. I know that this may sound a touch obvious, but I further qualify this by emphasising that it must very much be about cooking, together with skills, knowledge and an exactness of method. Helpful guidance not simply as to *why* certain dishes can be so enjoyable to cook, but also how wonderful they will taste if just a little time and trouble is taken in the kitchen. 'Cooking in more than an hour or so' – a working title in my head – may not, how shall we say, sell a concept, but it is, in general, how I work and what I do best.

This is not to say that I am unable to put together a pleasing plate of food in a very short time, or demonstrate such a thing to others.

However, I rarely think in terms of simply putting together three or four ingredients and calling it a recipe, but this idea seems to be the default way of many cooks *de nos jours*. There is nothing wrong with this, of course, but it has never exactly rocked my boat. I see this more as 'compiling', rather than integrating ingredients, thoughtfully introducing them to each other until harmoniously complete. This is the very crux of worthwhile cookery, I believe.

You may already know that this book developed from a TV series of the same name. In the planning of that series, we decided that it would be interesting to feature each programme as a 'menu'. Not as a restaurant menu, of course, but very much influenced by a little knowledge and experience over the years, as to how one balances such a thing. To domesticate this idea, it seemed appropriate to give each menu a descriptive name relating to a particular occasion, or reminiscence. A 'Sunday Roast', say, one of my most favourite lunches. Or a 'Continental Supper', which evolved around childhood memories of my first taste of a paella, for instance, on Spanish camping holidays during the 1960s. There is also a vegetarian menu, which later became 'A Touch of Spice', and remains my favourite.

The six chosen menus and a further six menus written especially for this book, begin with a fine cocktail or drink, together with a suitable nibble with which to enjoy them. This is then followed by a first course, a second course and a main dish and, finally, a dessert or traditional pudding. One's initial thought may well be that this is a lot of food! Well, it is. However, one must feel free and use simple judgement as to the kind of occasion one has in mind. The drink and nibble could go, for instance, or the middle course missed out; nothing here is set in stone. But I do think that these carefully constructed menus have a certain style to them, together with a seasonal nod and celebration of a particular occasion. It is the cook who is in charge, after all…

After over 40 years of almost constant cooking, suitably seasonal menus will pop into the head of this cook in a twinkling. This is not showing off, nor appearing to be glib; it is simply a matter of ease. And so it is down to this: I know not of any other profession than cookery, which is also seen as a daily, enjoyable chore in the home. Well, that is how it *used* to be seen. Sadly, there are now so many options for domestic cooking not to be a daily pleasure that it quietly depresses me. For all the books, articles, television programmes on food, as well as eating out in fancy restaurants, more and more people at home simply *do not cook*. An astonishing number of perfectly competent folk will even choose to buy a packet of cold roast potatoes or mashed potatoes to heat up, or even ready-made Yorkshire puddings and pancakes.

Yes, I too occasionally buy a Fray Bentos steak and kidney pie, for instance, because I have always liked them (although a new recipe with the moniker 'classic' on the tin is, sadly, not as good as the original I knew and loved). At each end of the eating curve I am as eternally fond of a fine serving of fish and chips as I am of an expertly made fruit tart from an artisan pastry shop. The domestic Parisian cook, for instance, is particularly proud of their knowledge of the finest *pâtisserie* within their *arrondissement*. After all, as these sensible folk know full well, such a skill is professional, rather than domestic, so competition is futile. But would they buy a 'sell-by-date' portion of *pommes purée*? *Jamais*!

I will also shop anywhere for that which aids and pleases me, culinary-wise. I am no snob. Yes, I love shopping at my local farmers' market where, as an example, I can buy a pot of untreated Guernsey cream unavailable anywhere else. But I will also regularly alternate between three local supermarkets in my manor, where there is both a thriving West Indian and a Polish community.

So, enterprisingly, I can buy a Polish brand of tomato juice (one of the best I have ever tasted) as well as a Polish loaf of bread with the lightest crumb, which makes the best toast ever. The lowliest supermarket of the three sells the freshest chicken livers I have ever seen offered in such a place. Even my local Costcutter shop takes into account that there are three French schools nearby. Hence there are good brands of bottled cornichons, Amora Dijon mustard (my favourite) and excellent puff pastry – which properly puffs! I am just making observations here, but it also helps to know that enterprise and care in the 'big shops' are, occasionally, on one's side.

Folk are often astonished when I answer the question, 'How often do you cook?' (in itself, a surprising question, I always think), with the following response: 'Every single day.' 'Really?', they say. 'Yes, every single day', I reply with emphasis. 'It is what I do.' Even when staying with close friends for a weekend, they know I will want to cook at some stage; two particularly close friends have very nice kitchens, which is a further boon.

I think that which some may find unusual is that I am a single man, so who eats all the food? Well, I don't cook dishes that feed the five thousand, but I also need to test recipes and make sure that they work; this is my job.

But, make no mistake, I love cooking for *me* as much as for anyone. I am not fond of doing 'dinner parties' much anymore, but I do enjoy a long lunch with a like-minded chum, whiling away a Saturday afternoon, say, with good wine and conversation. Also, friends and neighbours are always happy to receive takeaways...

Furthermore, and importantly, what with my fridge being constantly full of food, I know full well how long things keep, both before and after they have been cooked. This is also something that is not as understood as it once was, ever since the 'sell-by date' revolution took hold (and all that goes with that tricky subject), together with a diminishing lack of knowledge as shopping habits have changed. And I loathe waste! I learnt from my late mother how a leftover roast will make delicious rissoles; how a broth from a roast chicken carcass will be the basis of a fine soup; that all stale bread kept will make breadcrumbs. So, these are not tips I learnt in restaurants, but from growing up in a sensibly organised, thrifty domestic kitchen.

With this in mind, I urge you to shop carefully and with the spirit of an interested and keen cook. Read more about good cookery and use the books in the kitchen rather than at the coffee table! And *find* the time to make things right; you just know it makes sense. But, finally, I truly hope that you understand quite how keen I am to encourage and inspire you to cook with pleasure. It *is* my life – and wouldn't you like to make it a little more of your life, too?

Simon Hopkinson
September 2013

A continental supper

Negroni

·

Anchovies on toast

·

Green bean salad with shallots & cream

·

Gnudi

·

Paella

·

Coffee caramel custard

Menu introduction

As a child taking holidays with my parents and brother throughout the 1960s (mostly on the Costa Brava, but occasionally in Italy and France, too), the destination we were heading for was generally referred to as 'The Continent'. Over time, the description of this romantic journey would be dumbed down to just the one, rather more prosaic word: 'abroad'. 'Overseas' was another idealistic description, which possibly predated 'Continental' and at the time, might even have overlapped, depending upon a mix of social background and a legacy of post-war jargon. Mind you, these days when asking someone where they may be going for their holidays, the reply is often simply thus: 'Oh, you know, somewhere hot.'

It was a beautiful hot day in Venice where I sipped my very first, cooling negroni. Oh yes, the drink was packed with ice, but one could not exactly have called it refreshing. It is one of the most grown-up of cocktails; a heady mix of equal parts of gin, sweet vermouth and Campari, flavoured with the zest of an orange. It is truly special, but even more so when served by a handsome waiter bearing the drink upon a silver tray from the bar of Florian, the legendary coffee house on St Mark's Square.

To encapsulate the essence of a negroni, it is to Margot Henderson's terrific book *You're All Invited* (Fig Tree, 2012) to which I turn. She describes with fierce accuracy the effect of party negroni drinking: 'Wait for a few moments and then listen for the negroni roar once the room has consumed a jug or two.' And how right she is. To prevent imminent collapse at such a gathering, fuel oneself with crisp fingers of fried and toasted bread topped with a salty sliver of anchovy, the deeply savoury notes nicely cutting the drink. Almost – but possibly not quite – calming that growing roar.

Allow me to immediately inform the reader of personal pedantry regarding a long-standing, ongoing plea: please top *and* tail fine green beans. You know it makes sense. Once this is done, use this exacting green vegetable for salads in the French way: dressed while still just warm, served at room temperature and eaten as a course in itself rather than as an accompaniment to, say, a plate of grilled lamb cutlets; although, I might add, a pairing not to be dismissed out of hand. It is just that green beans can be so very delicious as a solo serving. And cook them a touch more than you might think; I believe that a bean that squeaks when you eat it is not a nice thing to experience.

I should here admit that the dish, gnudi, is relatively gnu to me. It cannot be more than about five years ago that I first ate a plateful of these at the west London restaurant The River Café, on yet another hot day. Outside on the sunny terrace, a glass of chilled Planeta chardonnay (from Sicily) to hand and yet another handsome waiter (from Richmond) sliding in front of me these remarkable ricotta dumplings, all deliciously doused in a new-season Tuscan olive oil, and nothing but these two ingredients on the plate. So brave. So insistent of the cook's intent. I choose to add butter and sage to my gnudi; maybe I'm a coward, or perhaps the olive oil I have at home is not quite up to scratch. Please have a go at making these little marvels – and only then decide how you wish to dress them up.

Thankfully, a Spanish paella has yet to succumb to the indignities that have fallen upon the Italian risotto in recent years (I saw chocolate and chilli, not so long ago...). I knew nothing of risotto when I forked up my first mouthful of paella when about 8 years old (Continental holiday dish number one), but then hardly anyone ate rice dishes in Britain at the time; rice pudding being, perhaps, the one exception – delicious when carefully made.

Both paella and risotto are dishes that are all about the rice. Although this is abundantly clear in the case of risotto (note the first three letters of the name), the paella is, in fact, named after the pan in which it is cooked. Nevertheless, rice remains entirely the reason for making a paella.

There are various regional recipes all over Spain, all argued over to be sure, but vigorously upheld by local cooks. I was once castigated in print with a letter from an outraged expat Brit, questioning my inclusion of chorizo sausage in a paella recipe. Since this ticking off, I have discovered that my apparently heretical addition was not the 'go-and-stand-in-the-corner' moment I had initially thought – and this information from a Spanish cook I absolutely trust.

The rice called 'bomba' is the most commonly used for making paella. Grown around the town of Calasparra, in Murcia, it is a tight, tough little grain and perfect for being able to soak up plenty of liquid as it cooks. In fact, the rice I usually buy is itself named 'Calasparra', and packaged in rather fetching, artisan-style cloth bags, so I have always thought it may well be the finest brand. Well, it has always performed impeccably for me.

However, I have also been informed (by the same Spanish cook) that Calasparra soaks up a little less liquid than bomba, so perhaps adjustments should be taken into account when rice and liquids are being measured.

And finally, to France, for an elegant finish to this Continental cornucopia! A *crème caramel au café*. To be frank, the English description of 'caramel custard' is one of which I have always been rather fond. My mother used to buy a ready-made packet version of this when I was a boy, and what a delicious treat was this. I haven't a clue as to where she used to buy it in Lancashire in the early 1960s, but find it she did; it certainly predated 'Angel Delight', that's for sure. The added coffee flavour in this recipe is, at once, subtle and sophisticated.

Negroni

SERVES 4

Mix together equal measures of gin, sweet vermouth and Campari over ice.

Add a strip of orange zest and stir.

Anchovies on toast

SERVES 4

olive oil
1 small loaf of pain de mie, sliced
12 anchovy fillets (such as the Ortiz brand)
cayenne pepper

Brush olive oil over one side of six slices of bread. Using three at a time, lay them oil-side down in a frying pan set over a moderate heat. Allow to become golden for a couple of minutes, while also using this time to brush oil on their other sides. Flip them over, repeat the process and keep warm. Now do the same to the remaining three slices.

Lay two anchovy fillets along the length of each slice of toast, allowing a gap between them. Cut off the crusts (or not, if you like) and slice between the anchovies to make two 'anchovy soldiers'. Sprinkle over a touch of cayenne and eat with the negroni.

Green bean salad with shallots and cream

SERVES 4

400–500g extra fine French green beans, topped and tailed
1 shallot, finely chopped
1 tbsp chopped parsley
a little olive oil

FOR THE DRESSING:
2 tsp smooth Dijon mustard
½ tbsp red wine vinegar, or to taste
1 small clove of garlic, crushed to a paste with a little sea salt
2 tbsp extra virgin olive oil
125ml whipping cream
freshly ground white pepper

To make the dressing, whisk together the mustard, vinegar, garlic, oil and pepper until smooth in a small bowl. Pour in the cream, continuing to whisk, until frothy and slightly thickened; do not over-mix or the cream will split. Tip into a roomy salad bowl and put to one side.

Fill a large pan with salted water and bring to a rolling boil. Drop in the beans and cook briskly for 4–5 minutes, or until tender but not at all crunchy; eat one if you are unsure. Drain in a colander and shake dry. Now tip the beans directly into the bowl of dressing and quickly toss together with the shallot and parsley until the beans are well coated. Leave the salad until lukewarm, then divide between four plates and trickle a little extra olive oil on to each serving.

Gnudi

SERVES 4

NOTE: THE RECIPE NEEDS TO BE STARTED THE DAY BEFORE YOU WISH TO COOK THE GNUDI.

500g fresh ricotta
100g freshly grated Parmesan
about a third of a nutmeg, grated
approx. 500g semolina
100g unsalted butter
about 20 sage leaves
salt and freshly ground black pepper
extra grated Parmesan to hand, at table

Put the ricotta, Parmesan and nutmeg into a bowl and beat together until smooth. Pour half the semolina into a shallow tray. Slightly wet the palms of your hands and briefly lay them in the semolina. Now take up a small piece of the ricotta mix (a large teaspoon, say), gently roll it into a ball about the size of a big marble and drop it into the semolina. Push the tray back and forth to fully coat the ball with semolina and continue this process until all the ricotta mixture is used up. Pour the rest of the semolina over the ricotta balls until they are well covered. Place in the fridge, covered, overnight.

•

The next day, carefully lift out the gnudi from the semolina and put on to a large plate lined with kitchen paper. Put a large, wide pot of lightly salted water on to boil (also, have four hot plates ready to hand). Meanwhile, start to melt the butter in a deep frying pan over a very low heat and switch off the heat when it has. Once the water boils, turn it down to a simmer and slide in the gnudi. Now turn up the heat a touch and patiently wait until the gnudi float to the surface, about 4–5 minutes. When all have risen, carefully lift them out (they are delicate) using a slotted spoon, draining them well, and divide equally between four hot plates. Turn the heat up under the melted butter and, when it is frothing, toss in the sage leaves, gently cook them until crisp, and without the butter becoming too brown; it should, however, smell nutty and look golden. Spoon immediately over the gnudi and serve without delay. Hand extra Parmesan at table for those who want it. Me.

Paella

SERVES 4

2 tbsp olive oil
1 small picante chorizo sausage (approx. 150g), skinned and cut into small pieces
1 medium squid, approximately 200g, cleaned
4 skinless, boneless chicken thighs, cut into small pieces
100ml dry sherry
200g cherry tomatoes
4 cloves of garlic
1 heaped tsp Spanish pimentón
150g stringless, flat green beans, thinly sliced
150g good-quality sweet red peppers from a jar, thickly sliced
1 tsp saffron threads
600ml hot chicken stock
300g Spanish bomba or Calasparra rice
750g mussels, debearded and well washed

TO FINISH THE PAELLA:
2–3 cloves of garlic, finely chopped
2 tbsp chopped parsley
4–5 tbsp olive oil
2 lemons, quartered

Using a large paella pan (I use one that is supposed to be for six, as I prefer the extra room in the pan), heat the oil and in it gently fry the chorizo until the fat runs. Lift it out with a slotted spoon and put on to a plate. Now introduce the squid and very briefly fry until lightly coloured. Remove and slice into thin rings. Add to the chorizo.

•

Lightly season the chicken in the same pan with salt and pepper, and cook until golden brown, for about 5 minutes. Meanwhile, put the sherry, tomatoes, garlic and pimentón into a liquidiser, process until very smooth then, using a small ladle, push through a fine sieve into a bowl (discard the solids). Once the chicken is well coloured add the tomato mixture to the pan and bring up to a simmer. Cook, uncovered, for about 15 minutes, stirring occasionally, until the tomato mixture has thickened – almost to a thin purée and a bit oily in parts.

•

Now add the beans, peppers and saffron. Reintroduce the chorizo and squid, and carefully pour in the chicken stock. Stir all together and bring up to a simmer once more. Sprinkle the rice into the liquid and stir in well, making sure that it is evenly distributed among the chicken pieces; once you have done this try not to stir the rice again. Cook the paella over a moderate heat for a good 20 minutes, or until you can see the rice puffing up between the chicken.

•

Now carefully push the mussels halfway into the rice hinge-side down, in any space you can fit them. Then cover with foil and put in the oven for 5 minutes at 180°C/gas mark 4.

Once the mussels have steamed through, remove the foil. Mix together the garlic, parsley and olive oil. Trickle over the paella, arrange the lemon quarters over the rice and serve it directly from the pan on to very hot plates; remember, rice dishes cool quickly. Dig deep to find the sticky, golden and a touch toasty rice in the bottom of the pan. This is called 'socorat'; it is the best bit of the paella and highly prized.

Coffee caramel custard

SERVES 4

NOTE: YOU WILL NEED 4 LARGE DARIOLE MOULDS OF APPROX. 175ML.

400ml full-fat milk
4 espresso coffees
a small carton of double cream
80g espresso coffee beans
pinch of salt
1/2 tsp vanilla extract
120g granulated sugar
3 eggs
4 egg yolks
75g caster sugar

Preheat the oven to 150°C/gas mark 2.

•

Pour the milk into a measuring jug and add the four espresso coffees. Now top up this mixture with double cream until it reaches 600ml. Pour into a stainless steel pan and add the coffee beans, salt and vanilla extract. Warm together, occasionally stirring, until just below simmering point. Switch off the heat, cover with a lid and leave to infuse for at least 2 hours.

•

Now put the granulated sugar in a heavy-based saucepan and add 3–4 tablespoons of water. Bring to a simmer and cook slowly until the sugar has become a richly coloured caramel; take care during the final stages, so as not to burn it. Pour into the base of the dariole moulds, dividing the caramel between them. Leave to cool.

•

Put the eggs, yolks and caster sugar into a roomy bowl. Whisk together lightly then strain over the coffee-infused milk (discard the exhausted beans). Gently whisk together (not vigorously) until well blended, then ladle the mixture into the caramel-lined moulds and fill to the brim. Place them in a deep roasting tin and fill with tap-hot water, so that it rises up the outside of the moulds by about three quarters. Carefully slide the tin into the oven and loosely lay a sheet of tin foil flat over the surface of the moulds, but **do not secure it down**. Bake in the oven until the custards are set, about 40–45 minutes To check when they are ready, lightly press a finger on the surface, or give them a little shake: they should wobble.

•

Remove from the oven, take out of the roasting tin and leave to cool. When quite cold, cover each custard with a small sheet of clingfilm and put in the fridge for at least three hours. To unmould, run a small knife around the edge of the custard and upend on to individual, shallow dishes. Eat with a teaspoon – and with great pleasure.

A classic lunch

Gin martini

·

Tiny fennel-salami sandwiches

·

Artichoke with mustard vinaigrette

·

Prawn cocktail

·

Roast leg of lamb with anchovy, rosemary & garlic

·

Gratin de Jabron

·

Sherry trifle

Menu introduction

The word 'classic' is a description that, while accurate, I am beginning to find a trifle tedious. It seems to be used willy-nilly for almost anything that is often little more than 10 years old. Oh well... perhaps I primly exaggerate. You see for me, a 'classic' has been around the block a few times and, precisely because of that well-honed journey, has earned its place as memorable and, how shall we say, even cherished. The dry martini is a case in point (although these days it is usually referred to as 'the gin martini', the majority of martinis now being fashioned using vodka, and so one has reluctantly acquiesced). It remains the perfect, absolutely clean cocktail – always 'straight up', for me. There should be nothing in the drink to cloud its absolute purity: gin, vermouth, ice and a twist of lemon zest. Maybe an olive or two, for those who like that kind of thing... I mind not whether the cocktail is shaken or stirred, just make it is as cold as can be.

But to use the moniker 'martini' when describing a drink that may well include gin, or vodka, but further involve interlopers such as chocolate, strawberries, lychees – or, I don't know, pencil shavings? – is detracting from the very essence of this perfect assembly. These are not martinis, they are a travesty, and impolite in respect of the original. But enough – and let us at least talk of something nice to nibble with this legendary tipple.

I have always adored a salami sandwich. There is something especially nice about eating thinly sliced buttered bread filled with intensely flavoured, cured pork meat. Wafer-thin slices of Parma ham, for instance, are delicious in themselves, either inside a sandwich or folded upon the surface of some toasted and buttered sourdough bread. However, the salty, astringent taste that is delivered from a very fine salami – *finocchiona*, in this case (a Tuscan salami that is flavoured with fennel seeds) – is one of the very finest of salamis, making it an especially tasty sandwich.

If we are going to describe a 'classic' as having an age about it, then a simply boiled, whole globe artichoke surely runs into the thousands of years. This luscious thistle (for that is the true genus) has been cooked, eaten and relished since Roman times – and possibly before that. When I first started cooking in restaurant kitchens about 40 years ago, the artichoke was hardly ever cooked and served in any other way than simply boiled – and often to death. In Britain, then, melted butter seemed the most popular lotion in which to dip the leaves and final 'heart'; in France an unctuous vinaigrette dressing was the more usual accompaniment. Both are quite delicious anywhere.

My friend Lindsey Bareham and I wrote a cookery book together concerning the next course, in 1997: *The Prawn Cocktail Years* was its title. We initially wanted to put together a series of memories and dishes that we had both enjoyed during the 1960s and '70s, although also recipes that celebrate earlier classics (there it is again...), such as nursery dishes that would have been enjoyed in the 1950s and before that, too; the chapter, in this case: 'The Gentlemen's Club'.

However, it is the prawn cocktail and its cherished attendants – coq au vin, Wiener schnitzel, snails in garlic butter (*so* sophisticated, *so* daring!), sole Véronique, trout with almonds, saltimbocca alla romana, rhum baba and, of course, Black Forest gateau – that make up the bulk of the book. But the titular dish – that extraordinarily delicious, though simple assembly of shredded lettuce, prawns and pink cocktail sauce (sometimes known, rather kitschly, as 'sauce Marie Rose') remains, without question, one of my most favourite things to eat. Many of those I enjoyed in hotel dining rooms growing up (generous parents) may even have been fashioned from tinned prawns, and with the pink sauce decanted from a half-gallon catering tub. But, what the hell, once doused in that so comforting blanket of gloop, I slurped it down for England! The recipe I give here, however, is just a touch more palatable... Also, the addition of diced cucumber and spring onion offers further joy to this little gem, if I may say.

It would be about 20 years ago, now, that I first roasted a leg of lamb with anchovy, garlic and rosemary. It is possibly one of my most loved dishes, and is further endorsed by friends who have eaten it – so much so, that they have since gone on to cook it for themselves. I cannot recall for the life of me where the provenance originated (I have always assumed that it was from something I had read in a book by Elizabeth David, but have since failed ever to find any firm evidence of this), but I have somehow always been convinced that this magical trio would transform roast lamb into a tour de force. Interested cooks know full well how very nicely anchovies will flavour meat, as opposed to fish.

Partnered with fish, the salted anchovy will almost make it taste stale – even slightly 'off' – whereas with meat, it purely acts as a subversive seasoning; both elusive and intriguing. This is mainly to do with the slow salting process, which produces a deeply savoury flavour that no longer possesses the character of the original fish; just taste a fresh anchovy and the transformation becomes quite clear. Think Thai fish sauce, which when first sniffed smells kind of rotten, yet when used to season a dish simply becomes part of the whole. But with lamb, in particular, the anchovy plays its part superbly well.

My old friend Shaun Hill learnt to make a 'gratin de Jabron' when he was a young whipper-snapper chef working at The Capital Hotel, in London's Knightsbridge, sometime in the 1970s. Essentially, it is a variation on the well-known 'gratin Dauphinois'. The 'Jabron' recipe favours already-cooked potatoes before dairy ingredients are introduced, making the dish both more fondant and, perhaps, homely. When I saw Shaun recently, he said he had absolutely no idea of the origins of the recipe name, 'Jabron'. I was equally ignorant, too. Perhaps it really can be bliss.

And for pudding, a superb sherry trifle – and what could be more classic than that?

Gin martini

300ml good gin
(Plymouth is my favoured tipple)
50ml dry vermouth
(Dry Martini or Noilly Prat, if you prefer)
plenty of ice, briefly rinsed
4 strips of zest taken from an unwaxed lemon
(use a potato peeler)

First of all, have the gin in the fridge and glasses ready-chilled in the freezer; I use small glass beakers, inspired by those used at Harry's Bar in Venice. Now fill a large cocktail shaker (or glass jug) with plenty of ice. Add the vermouth and then pour over the gin. Mix well with a stirrer (I often use a chopstick) for about a minute, so that it is *really* cold. Strain into the chilled glasses and tweak the lemon zest over each glass using both thumbs and forefingers, outer skin facing down. Once you see the lemony oil spray over the surface of the drinks, discard the zest. Serve without delay.

Tiny fennel-salami sandwiches

SERVES 4

1 small loaf of bread, thinly sliced
(preferably with a close-textured crumb; for best results I use
pain de mie, which will slice nice and thin)
softened unsalted butter
about 12 thin slices fennel salami (finocchiona)
freshly ground black pepper

Cut the first, thick crusty slice of bread from one end of the loaf. Now, holding the loaf in one hand, thinly butter the newly exposed bread. Only now cut the first thin slice and lay out on a chopping or bread board. Continue until you have seven more buttered slices. Now, cover four of them with three slices each of salami (carefully folding them over so that they neatly fit the bread) and grind over plenty of black pepper. Lay over the other four slices and press firmly to seal together. Cut off the crusts, then cut each sandwich into four dainty fingers. Serve with the martinis, whilst also marvelling at how deliciously they complement each other.

Artichoke with mustard vinaigrette

SERVES 4

a good glug of pure olive oil (not extra virgin)
a lesser glug of white wine vinegar
a small glass of white wine
1/2 tbsp fine salt
2 bay leaves
4 large globe artichokes, trimmed and well rinsed in water

FOR THE DRESSING:
1 tbsp smooth Dijon mustard
1/2 tbsp red wine vinegar, or to taste
1 small clove of garlic, crushed to a paste with a little sea salt
75ml extra virgin olive oil
125ml sunflower oil
freshly ground white pepper

Into a stainless steel pan (*never* aluminium, which will taint the flavour of the artichokes) that will comfortably accommodate the artichokes, put the oil, vinegar, wine, salt and bay. Now pop in the artichokes and just cover with cold water. Bring up to a simmer and cook for about 40 minutes, partially covered; if they are less than large, 25–30 minutes should be sufficient. Check that they are done by pulling away an artichoke leaf about halfway down; if it eases away with just the slightest resistance, the artichoke is cooked.

Lift out the artichokes with a slotted spoon and drain upside down in a colander until lukewarm, preferably, rather than stone cold.

To make the dressing, put the mustard, vinegar, garlic and pepper into a small food processor, then add a tablespoon of water from a kettle that has been off the boil for about 15 minutes. Whizz together until smooth, then add a glug or two of olive oil. Whizz again until the oil has been incorporated. Add a bit more, and continue whizzing. Now add the sunflower oil and proceed until both oils have been used up. If the dressing is far too thick, loosen with a touch more hot water; the consistency should be that of salad cream.

To serve, place each artichoke on a large plate (to leave room for discarded leaves) and hand the mustard vinaigrette at table, with finger bowls.

Prawn cocktail

SERVES 4

NOTE: YOU WILL NEED 4 BIG GLASSES.

the hearts of 2 Little Gem lettuces, finely shredded
4–5 tbsp mayonnaise (see below)
1–2 tbsp tomato ketchup, or to taste
3–4 shakes Tabasco sauce
a dribble or two of cognac
2 spring onions, trimmed and thinly sliced
¼ small cucumber, peeled, deseeded and finely diced
400g cooked, shell-on prawns, heads removed and peeled
4 small lemon wedges
touch of paprika

FOR THE MAYONNAISE:
2 egg yolks
2 tsp smooth Dijon mustard
300ml sunflower or other neutral oil
juice of ½ large lemon
150ml extra virgin olive oil (fragrant, but not strongly flavoured)
salt and freshly ground white pepper

Begin with the mayonnaise. Put the egg yolks into a roomy bowl and mix in the mustard and a little seasoning. Beginning slowly, whisk together, while very slowly trickling in the sunflower oil. Once the mixture is becoming very thick, add a little lemon juice. Continue beating, adding the oil a little faster and increasing the beating speed. Once the oil has been used up, add some more lemon juice and then begin incorporating the olive oil until you are happy with the taste. Now add a final squeeze of lemon juice if you think it necessary. Finally, taste for seasoning, spoon into a lidded plastic pot and keep in the fridge until ready to use.

Put the shredded lettuce in a small bowl, cover with cold water and a few cubes of ice; this will crisp the lettuce. Leave for a few minutes while you make the cocktail sauce. In another bowl, mix together the mayonnaise, ketchup, Tabasco and cognac; the sauce should be regulation pink. Fold in the spring onions and cucumber. Put to one side.

•

Drain the lettuce and either spin-dry, or place on a tea towel, gently roll it up and then tip out into a bowl. Divide the lettuce into the bottom of four big glasses, top with the prawns, dividing them equally between each glass, then spoon over the cocktail sauce, allowing it to completely cover the prawns.

Carefully slide a sharp knife between the skin and flesh of the lemon wedges, but cutting only halfway through. Attach these to the rim of each glass and sprinkle the cocktail with a touch of paprika. Brown bread and butter is, I feel, essential here.

Roast leg of lamb with anchovy, rosemary and garlic

SERVES 4, WITH SECONDS...

1.8–2kg leg of lamb, on the bone, trimmed
2 x 50g tins of anchovies in olive oil, drained
a bunch of rosemary, the soft variety rather than spiky
4–5 large cloves of garlic, peeled and sliced
75g softened butter
½ a bottle of dry white wine
juice of 1 lemon
watercress, to garnish
a little salt and plenty of black pepper

Preheat the oven to 220°C/gas mark 7.

•

Using a small, sharp knife, make about a dozen or more incisions into the lamb, especially deep down into the most fleshy, top part of the leg. Using your little finger, widen the incisions to allow you to insert half an anchovy, a small sprig of rosemary and a slice of garlic. Cream the butter with any anchovy fillets left over (there may not be any) and smear it all over the lamb. Salt very lightly and grind over plenty of black pepper. Place the joint in a roasting tin and pour the wine around it. Squeeze over a little lemon juice and add any leftover sprigs of rosemary (there will be). Put into the oven and roast for 20 minutes.

•

Now, turn the oven down to 180°C/gas mark 4 and roast the lamb for a further hour or so, depending upon how you like your lamb: these timings should offer nice pink meat, once rested. Baste from time to time with the winey juices. Once ready, remove the joint from the oven (switch it off and leave the door ajar), transfer to a carving dish, cover with foil and after about 5 minutes return it to the waning heat of the oven to rest, still with the door ajar.

•

Taste the juices in the roasting tin and see if any further salt is needed (there shouldn't be). During the roasting process the wine will have reduced somewhat and mingled nicely with the meat juices (there will be more juices surrounding the meat in the oven, once fully rested) and the butter.

•

To serve, remove the lamb from the oven and add the juices from the carving dish to the roasting tin. Put the tin directly on to a moderate flame and bubble the juices, scraping any bits from around the tin. Strain into a small pan and reheat, skimming off any unsightly scum that forms in the process, then pour into a previously warmed gravy boat or jug. Carve the lamb into thickish slices and serve with watercress and the following gratin de Jabron. Personally, I don't believe that any other accompaniment is necessary here.

Gratin de Jabron

1kg medium-sized potatoes (Maris Piper are good here)
100g unsalted butter
3 cloves of garlic, peeled, crushed and chopped
200ml milk and 300ml whipping cream, mixed together
salt and freshly ground white pepper

Preheat the oven to 180°C/gas mark 4.

•

Steam the potatoes until they are nearly cooked but still a little firm in the middle; about 40 minutes. Remove from the steamer and allow to cool for several minutes.

•

Melt the butter with the garlic in a small pan and allow to bubble a bit, without letting it sizzle. Now, take an oval baking dish (approx. 30 x 20cm, or slightly larger) and spoon all the garlic with a little of the butter, all over the base of the dish, while also spreading it about a bit. Peel the potatoes and cut them into thickish slices; don't worry if some break up a little or if the slices are not precisely identical with regard to thickness. Arrange in the dish with each slice of potato overlapping the previous one until the dish is full. Now dribble the remaining butter over the potatoes and season with salt and pepper. Pour over the milk and cream and then bake for about 40 minutes, or until golden, bubbling and richly creamy.

Sherry trifle

SERVES 4, WITH PLENTY OF SECOND HELPINGS...
NOTE: YOU WILL NEED A LOOSE-BOTTOMED CAKE TIN, APPROX 18 X 4CM.

raspberry jam
125ml amontillado sherry
250g frozen raspberries

FOR THE SPONGE CAKE:
2 eggs, weighed in their shells
the weight of the eggs in:
softened salted butter, plus a little extra
for greasing the cake tin
caster sugar
self-raising flour, sifted
1 level tsp baking powder

FOR THE CUSTARD:
150ml full-fat milk
200ml double cream
6 egg yolks
1 tbsp caster sugar
1 tsp vanilla extract

TO FINISH THE TRIFLE:
300ml double cream
1 tbsp caster sugar
crystallised violets

Preheat the oven to 180°C/gas mark 4.

•

Start by making the sponge. In the bowl of an electric mixer (or use a hand-held electric mixer), whisk the eggs until frothy then add the other ingredients all at once and beat until thick and pale; the mixture should *just* flop off the whisk and should be of a dropping consistency. Line the base of a small (approx. 18 x 4cm), non-stick and loose-bottomed cake tin with a circle of baking parchment and grease the sides with butter. Pile in the sponge mix, level it off with a spatula and bake for about 30–35 minutes, or until springy to the touch of a finger. Remove from the oven and leave in the tin for a minute or two, then turn out on to a cake rack. Remove the parchment and leave to cool.

Cut the sponge cake into small, thick fingers and spread with raspberry jam. Arrange in the base of a glass bowl (approx. 2 litres capacity) and pour over the sherry. Sprinkle over the frozen raspberries (frozen are best here, as their juice will also soak into the sponge as they defrost). Put to one side while you make the custard.

•

To make the custard, warm the milk and cream in a pan over a low heat. Beat together the egg yolks, sugar and vanilla extract until frothy. Add the milk to the yolk mixture and whisk together. Return to the pan and, using a wooden spoon, stir over a very low heat until it begins to thicken; watch it carefully, and alternate between the spoon and a whisk, to prevent scrambling the custard. The finished look of the custard should be wobbly and thick. Immediately pour it over the sponge and raspberries, then shake the bowl a little to allow the custard to seep down within the pieces of sponge. Leave to cool for 10 minutes, then place in the fridge so that the custard firms up – at least 2 hours or so.

•

To finish the trifle, whip together the cream and sugar until loosely thick (take care not to over-whip) and pile on to the set custard. Smooth the surface and decorate with the crystallised violets.

A touch of spice

A glass of ouzo
·
Hummus
·
Ajo blanco
·
Aubergines with ginger, spring onions & red chilli
·
New tomato curry
·
Cucumber raita
·
Lemon pilau rice
·
Italian fruit & nut tart

Menu introduction

I was introduced to the Greek aniseed drink ouzo by my friend Fay Maschler, while staying with her and her husband, Reg, at their house in the Mani, on the Greek mainland – the Peloponnese, to be exact. It was about 10 years ago now, and I enjoyed my initial ice-cooled glass after a quite fabulous swim off the rocks which, conveniently, were hard by a simple taverna. Once invigorated by the big blue sea, I then quickly settled down at the table in damp swimming shorts and beach towel, while also glancing hungrily at a plate of various meze. I took my first sip and it was wonderful. This was surprising, only because I had never before been able to grasp the allure of the similarly aniseed-scented glass of pastis while sitting outside the Café de Flore, that iconic literary café on the boulevard Saint Germain on the Left Bank in Paris, where this drink is almost de rigueur. Much though I enjoy the flavour of aniseed in food – dill, tarragon, delicate chervil, fennel seeds – I had never reconciled myself to the taste of that perfect, early evening French apéritif. But here in Greece, the spell surrounding my aversion was finally broken by that first glass of ice-cold ouzo. So, thank you, Fay, for flicking that switch all those years ago… And, now I may also embrace a glass of '51' (my favourite pastis) along with the beau monde at the Café de Flore, and feel very much à la maison.

Ah… hummus. Another first, this time with my brother Jerry, in a tiny Greek-Cypriot joint (not much more than a front room) close to Warren Street tube station, in London. It was SO cheap that it beggared belief – and strapped for cash as I was, in 1974, this was a good thing. We had some taramasalata, too, with each generous and delicious paste served on cheap dolly-mixture pastel picnic plates. The toasted pitta with them was also a new bread to me, and memorably enjoyed by dragging torn pieces through these intensely savoury novelties. I seem to recall that the entire account for this late supper – including lamb kebabs as well – amounted to not much more than two to three of our English pounds. As to the following recipe for my 'best ever' hummus, I urge you to allow time to peel the chickpeas, a relatively recent suggestion by a close chum, who loves making and eating hummus just as much as I do.

Some say that ajo blanco (garlic-white, literally) may well be the original gazpacho: fresh almonds pounded together with garlic and olive oil, salt and vinegar, together with cold water to thin it to a drinkable mix. It should be taken as cold as possible and, it is thought, would have cooled the brow of the Spanish worker toiling under the blazing sun amongst olive grove, vineyard and, of course, beneath the almond tree. The version that follows is based upon one that Bibendum's kitchen produced on a hot day in the summer of 2012. Especially good was the beautiful garnish of pure-white, fresh almond slivers.

The delightful second-course dish of aubergines is rooted in Japanese cooking. The first time that I ate a version of this was in a modern-style, quasi-Japanese restaurant, where it was cooked over a charcoal grill, the smoking embers giving the vegetable's tender skin a deliciously charred flavour. I love its sweet and salty taste, together with a mild hit of chilli, which is my own addition to the original concept. For best results, try to search out long and slender Asian aubergines, with their thin lilac-coloured skins, as these perform particularly well with regard to this recipe.

I first cooked a tomato curry several years ago after visiting an Indian vegetarian restaurant (now sadly closed) in South London's Tooting, where a tomato curry was their speciality. Moreover, it was not only vegetarian, it was owned by a family who were of the Jain religion; no roots or tubers are cooked or consumed, and many other culinary restrictions are observed. To make a curry without the use of, particularly, onions and garlic is a challenge, but this more recent and more authentic recipe of mine (meticulously devised and honed) and with respect to Jain cookery, has turned out rather nicely and is, I think, as near to the original as memory allows – certainly in terms of taste.

A lovely cooling contrast to the heat of the curry (the fresh green peppercorns are entirely responsible for this) is a fragrant raita – and please don't use Greek yoghurt to make it, as this will be too thick and creamy. Raita is one of the most delicious side dishes in Indian cookery and is, as far as I am concerned, an essential tracklement to *all* curries.

I used to be pathetically inept at cooking rice. However, over recent years I have forced myself to improve my technique. One of the most important points to remember when making a pilau (or pilaf) is the ratio of liquid to rice. Many make the mistake – as I used to do – of doubling the volume (or weight) of rice to water/stock. Stick to one-and-a-half times liquid to rice and you won't go wrong. Trust me on this and you will produce a wonderfully light and fragrant pot of pilau every single time. Note: I only ever use Tilda basmati rice (in a blue and silver bag) and *never* wash it.

Jeremy Lee (chef at London's Quo Vadis restaurant), when he worked in the kitchen at Bibendum some 20 years ago, used to make the origin of the wonderful tart that rounds off this menu when he made occasional forays in to the pastry section. It was always a treat when it emerged from the oven all puffed, crisp and smelling quite divine; the unique fragrance of it, in fact, would herald its arrival on Jeremy's work station. 'Ah', I would proclaim, 'your lovely tart again, dear heart!' Always a sell-out, this delicious little number. We begin this menu with almonds and end it with them, too. And I think that's rather nice, don't you?

A glass of ouzo

MAKES 4

12–16 ice cubes
enough ouzo for 4

Place 3–4 ice cubes in four thin, tall glasses and pour over a healthy glug or two of ouzo. Top up with cold water – or not – as desired, and stir well.

Hummus

MAKES ABOUT 350G, PLENTY FOR 4 DIPPERS

230g canned or bottled chickpeas (drained weight but save the cooking liquid)
75g tahini
3–4 tbsp chickpea cooking liquid
1 large clove of garlic, crushed to a paste with 1 tsp sea salt
2 tbsp lemon juice
½ tsp ground cumin

TO SERVE:
best olive oil
toasted pitta bread

Put the chickpeas into a tea towel, fold it over and rub the chickpeas together to partially release their skins. Sadly, however, this will not be enough to remove every single skin and, infuriatingly, it seems that some peas have more than one! What one needs to achieve is a shiny look to the peeled pea, so any opaque skins remaining need removing with the fingers using a quick pinch. Ten minutes deleted from one's life for the best, most smooth hummus ever. Too much to ask? If it is, I suggest buying some ready-made and turning the page...

•

Put all the ingredients into a small food processor and blend until smooth, occasionally scraping down the sides as necessary. Decant, using a rubber spatula, into a pretty shallow bowl, trickle some olive oil over the surface and hand round some toasted pitta bread cut into soldiers.

Ajo blanco

SERVES 4

200g whole, skinned almonds
6 cloves of garlic, peeled, inner green germ removed if necessary, and crushed
1 cucumber, peeled and chopped into chunks
100g fresh white breadcrumbs
500ml ice-cold water, plus a little more if necessary
2 tsp sea salt
300ml extra virgin olive oil (the finer the oil, the better), plus a little extra to serve
2–3 tbsp sherry vinegar, to taste
1 green jalapeño chilli, deseeded (optional)
quince jelly, to serve

Put the almonds in a frying pan and place over a low heat. Shaking them around a bit, allow the almonds to gild slightly; the palest, very palest tinge is all that is necessary, just to accentuate the taste of the nut. Tip on to a plate and leave to cool.

•

Put all the ingredients (apart from the extra oil and quince jelly) into a large bowl and stir together. Have another large bowl – or, even better, a large Tupperware container – handy, with a fine sieve suspended over it. Now, using a large ladle, decant 2–3 ladles of the mixture at a time into a liquidiser, process until very smooth indeed, then pour into the sieve. Press each blending into the chosen container beneath, forcing through every last drop of liquid with the ladle. Once finished, taste the soup and whisk in any further seasonings/ acidity/oil you might think necessary to suit your personal taste. Cover and chill in the fridge for at least 2 hours, together with four soup bowls.

•

To serve, decant the soup into the chilled bowls, drop 5–6 tiny spoonfuls of jelly into each serving and, finally, trickle a little olive over the surface.

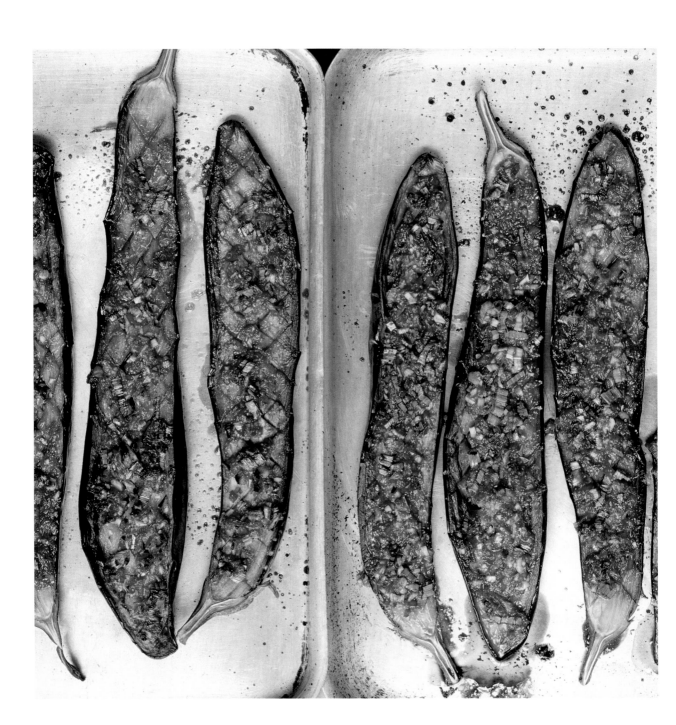

Aubergines with ginger, spring onions and red chilli

SERVES 4

200ml mirin (sweetened rice wine)
50ml light soy sauce
1 large knob of fresh ginger, peeled and finely grated
4 spring onions, trimmed and finely chopped
2 cloves of garlic, finely chopped
1 tbsp sesame oil
2 red chillies, deseeded and finely chopped
4 long purple Asian aubergines (approx. 600g)
peanut oil or other neutral-flavoured oil

Pour the mirin into a saucepan, bring up to the boil, then simmer until reduced to about half its original volume. Decant into a bowl and allow to cool completely. Add the next six ingredients and stir together.

Preheat the oven to 220°C/gas mark 7.

To prepare the aubergines, cut them in half lengthways and lightly score their surfaces with a sharp knife in a criss-cross fashion – don't go too deep. Heat a couple of tablespoons of the peanut oil in a large frying pan until hot, but not smoking. Lower in the aubergines cut-side down and fry until the flesh is golden (you will have to do this in batches, together with more oil); it will take about 3 minutes. Now turn them over and cook for about the same time, skin-side down. Drain well on kitchen paper, cut-side down, then place them on to a heatproof, shallow baking tray, cut-side uppermost.

Now, carefully spoon over about half the dressing, dividing it as you go between each aubergine. Place in the oven (top shelf) for 5 minutes. Remove, and add more dressing. Continue to bake the aubergines until very tender and almost drenched in the aromatic dressing; residue will also have collected in the baking tray, which will have further become deliciously brown and sticky. Flash under a hot grill to add extra gilding, if you so wish.

New tomato curry

1 tbsp cumin seeds
1 tbsp coriander seeds
10 cardamom pods
½ tbsp fennel seeds
½ tbsp black mustard seeds
6 cloves
2 star anise
2 tbsp sunflower oil or other neutral-flavoured oil
½ tsp ground turmeric
1 tsp sea salt
400ml coconut milk
2 tsp tamarind paste
a small handful of curry leaves
12 medium-sized tomatoes
2 branches of fresh green peppercorns
1–2 tsp sugar, depending on the sweetness of the tomatoes
6-7 healthy sprigs of coriander, leaves chopped

Using a frying pan, lightly toast the first seven whole spices until aromatic; take care that they don't scorch, however.

Heat the oil in a wide, shallow pan and add the whole spices. Fry for a couple of minutes over a moderate heat, then add the turmeric and salt. Pour in the coconut milk and stir in the tamarind and curry leaves. Bring up to a simmer and allow to cook quietly for about 15 minutes. Now, using a stick blender, blitz the mixture for about 30 seconds, just to break up the spices. Remove from the heat and leave to infuse while you skin and core the tomatoes and remove the peppercorns from their branches.

Pass the coconut sauce through a fine sieve and return it to the (washed up) pan. Put the tomatoes into the sauce (removed-core-side down) and sprinkle in the peppercorns. Allow the tomatoes to simmer in the sauce until softened and the sauce has reduced and become a touch thicker; about 15-20 minutes. Finally, taste the sauce to see if it needs a touch of sugar, or more salt, then stir in the chopped coriander leaves and serve forthwith.

Cucumber raita

SERVES 4

1 large cucumber, peeled
1 tsp salt
300g plain yoghurt
a little lemon juice
1 clove of garlic, crushed and finely chopped
1 green chilli, deseeded and finely chopped
1 heaped tbsp finely chopped mint

Coarsely grate the cucumber and sprinkle over the salt. Mix well, put into a colander and suspend over a deep bowl. Leave the cucumber to soak and drip for about 30 minutes – or a bit longer, it matters not. Manually squeeze out excess moisture from the cucumber, then place it in a bowl and mix in the yoghurt, lemon juice, garlic, chilli and mint. Decant into a serving dish and chill in the fridge for at least 30 minutes before serving.

Lemon pilau rice

SERVES 4

40g butter, plus an extra small knob
1 small onion, finely chopped
200g basmati rice (I always use Tilda and don't wash it)
320ml water
1 bay leaf
1 small lemon, zest removed in thin strips using a potato peeler, and the juice
squeezed into a small jug
salt and freshly ground white pepper

Preheat the oven to 180°C/gas mark 4.

•

Melt the butter in a roomy pot that also has a tight-fitting lid. Add the onion and cook gently until lightly coloured. Tip in the rice and stir around a bit in the butter and onion until well coated. Pour in the water, add the bay and slowly bring up to a simmer. Meanwhile, finely cut the strips of lemon zest into small slivers and pop in the pot, together with a little salt and pepper. Once the rice is simmering, put on the lid and slide into the oven. Cook for 15 minutes.

Remove from the oven, **don't lift off the lid**, and leave to sit for 5 minutes. Now take off the lid, and fluff up the rice with a fork while also pouring in the lemon juice. Lay a tea towel over the pan and then clamp the lid on tight. Leave be for another 5 minutes; this allows the rice to steam, which will then be absorbed by the towel. Finally, remove the lid and towel – *wonderful* fragrance emanating – and stir in the knob of butter to glisten the rice.

Italian fruit and nut tart

SERVES 4

200g ready-rolled, all-butter puff pastry
100g butter, softened, plus a little extra
75g caster sugar
125g ground almonds
50g plain flour
1 large egg (a large duck egg, in fact, would be perfect here)
grated zest of 1 orange
grated zest of ½ lemon
a little grated nutmeg
1 tbsp Marsala
1 tbsp Limoncello
60g crystallised orange peel (bought already chopped)
60g plain chocolate chips
40g pine kernels
a little icing sugar
cold, thick cream, to serve

Roll the pastry out a little more thinly and with it line a 20 x 3cm, well-buttered tart tin. Trim the pastry edge, but leave it slightly raised above the rim of the tin, as it will shrink a little during the cooking. Also, prick the base of the pastry all over with a fork. Place in the fridge to rest until the filling is ready. Note: there is no need to bake the pastry blind for this recipe – and how nice is that!

Preheat the oven to 190°C/gas mark 5; also, have a flat baking tray ready in the oven, too, which will help to cook the base of the pastry.

Electrically beat together the butter and caster sugar until really light and fluffy; about 5 minutes beating on full speed. Turn down the speed a little and briefly beat in the ground almonds and flour until blended in, then beat in the egg as well. Now, using a rubber spatula, fold in the two zests, nutmeg, Marsala, Limoncello, orange peel and chocolate chips (do **not** add the pine kernels, yet).

Remove the tin from the fridge and fill with the almond paste mixture. Now sprinkle over with the pine kernels. Slide into the oven, on to the pre-heated oven tray, and bake for 5 minutes. Turn the heat down to 180°C/gas mark 4 and bake for a further 30–35 minutes, until the filling has puffed up, the pine kernels are golden and the whole thing smells divine. Remove the tart, dust with sifted icing sugar, then return to the oven for 2–3 minutes until the sugar has slightly glazed. Leave to cool for about 15 minutes then remove from the tin. Best eaten warm, with cold, thick cream.

A sunday roast

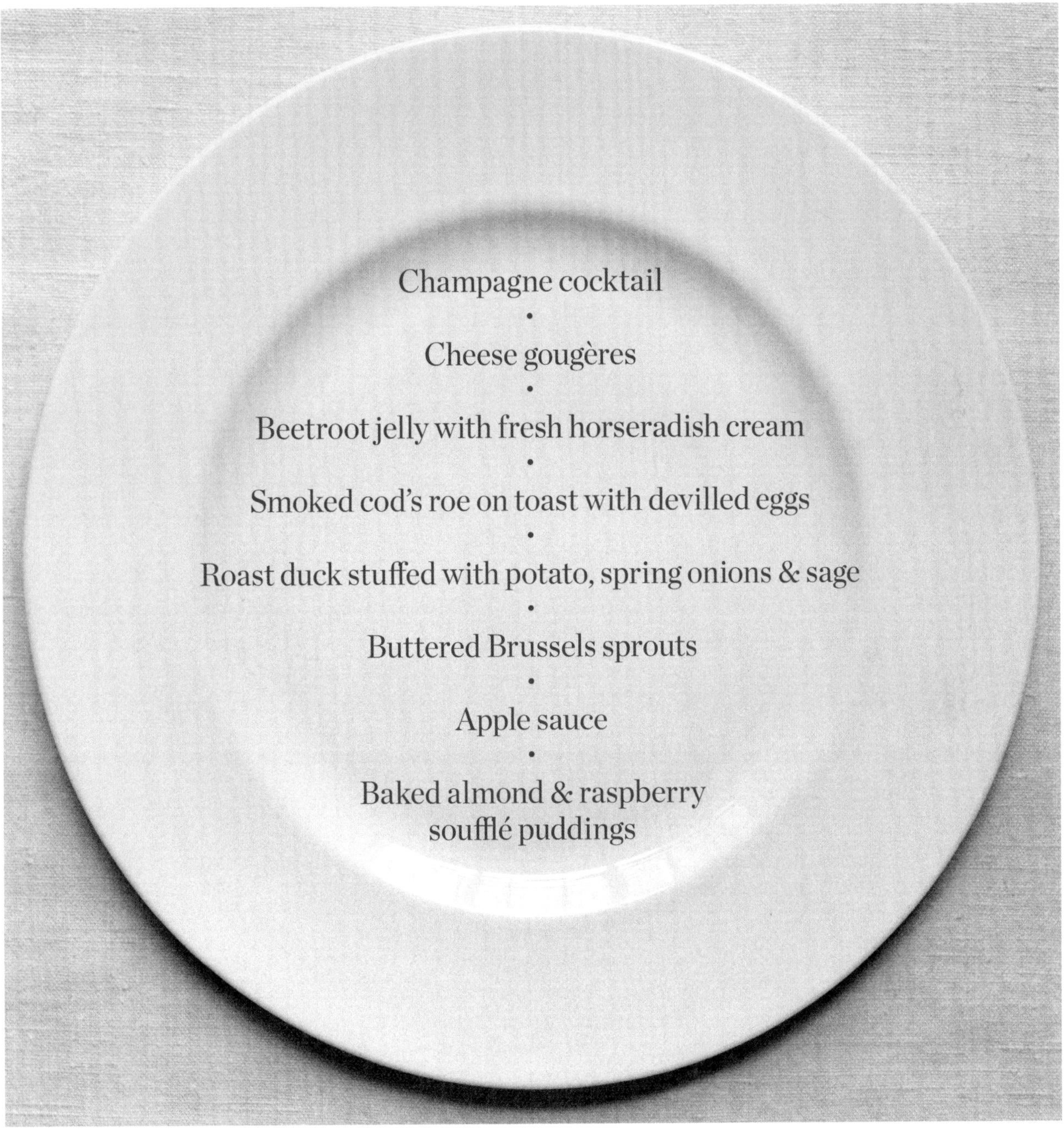

Champagne cocktail

·

Cheese gougères

·

Beetroot jelly with fresh horseradish cream

·

Smoked cod's roe on toast with devilled eggs

·

Roast duck stuffed with potato, spring onions & sage

·

Buttered Brussels sprouts

·

Apple sauce

·

Baked almond & raspberry
soufflé puddings

Menu introduction

A traditional Sunday lunch is seen as more of a treat, these days, than simply a happy, weekly occurrence. This is tragic, as I feel it is the one time of the week when a family – or just chums gathered together – can indulge in a veritable feast, and it is probably best to advise having that hearty, cooked weekend breakfast on Saturday, rather than spoil the appetite here. For me, and anyone else who enjoys this time-honoured tradition, Sunday lunch will always, but always, be a roast.

However, this particular Sunday lunch menu is a special one, involving my particular favourite indulgences, and is perhaps not necessarily for the faint-hearted. Of course, one doesn't *have* to serve all four dishes, but I think they balance out well and also celebrate an English flavour throughout. That is, apart from the openers...

A champagne cocktail is such a grand way to kick off a lavish lunch that it seemed only reasonable to give a kindly nod to France – and to one place in particular. My version is based on a cocktail served at the Oustau de Baumanière, a fabulous hotel and restaurant in Provence. That which makes it so very good indeed is the simple fact of adding ice to the mix. Quite simply, this keeps the drink as chilled as possible to the very last drop, so it is truly refreshing and lighter in taste than the standard, ice-free model.

For me, there is nothing worse than a champagne cocktail half drunk (the drink, not the imbiber), where the remains have become rather dreary, room-temperature dregs. For however ice-cold the champagne, once it hits the cognac, sugar lump and Angostura bitters it warms up pretty damn quick. With this particular recipe, the additional orange flavours also add a zesty freshness.

However, be warned, the cocktail remains as potent as ever, so I am serving some delectable

little cheese 'gougères' alongside, offering some much-needed ballast. Nevertheless, they are dainty, puffed-up and quietly seasoned with Gruyère cheese, and are the perfect accompaniment. So, do please eat lots of them if you wish to remain upright...

I am exceptionally fond of making clear, savoury jellies. This will always begin as a consommé (usually chicken, but occasionally beef), then may be flavoured with particular vegetables or herbs; tomato is a summer favourite, for example, and especially fine when scented with basil. However, the savoury jelly that appears in my kitchen more than any other, is one flavoured with beetroot. It may take a little time and effort to produce this exquisite little number; make it on perhaps what might, initially, have been a lazy Saturday afternoon... I also happen to think that a horseradish cream with which to serve the jelly is essential. The contrast is noteworthy.

I see the diminutive middle course as almost a frivolity, but it is truly delicious: a very Victorian smear of a little devilled egg and a splendid slice of smoked cod's roe (from the Cley smokehouse, in north Norfolk, in this case, and very good it is too) – and that's it. I suppose you could also swap the jelly and the cod's roe dish around, if you wished to, but do please at least try the smoked roe sometime; it is particularly nice all on its own as a Sunday supper. Make more, if this alternative is taken.

And now to the centrepiece of the lunch: a traditional roast duck. By this I mean well cooked, with crisp skin and soft, tender, almost fondant, meat – rarely seen, in these days of pink duck breast and the ubiquitous 'confit' (although quite delicious when carefully prepared). In fact, I know of only two hostelries, both in the Home Counties (Bucks and Berks), that specialise in cooking a proper roast duck (dear reader, I would love to know of others!). And, as far as I know, each establishment employs the English Aylesbury breed (I am reliably informed that this ancient breed has an ancestry dating back to the late 1700s). This remains *the* duck for a traditional roast, as far as this cook is concerned. So, do try and search out a duck that, at least, has an association with the Aylesbury breed and has been 'dry-plucked' rather than wet (wax and hot water are used here, I believe, producing a damp and flabby skin). Incidentally, I have sadly never had any real success with the increasingly common Gressingham duck, traditionally roasted, as its skin never seems to become as crisp as that of the Aylesbury bird.

Rather less traditionally English is the stuffing I use. Based upon an Irish recipe, it is, not surprisingly, made from potatoes. It was the grandmother of the late, great Peter Langan (founder of London's Langan's Brasserie) who was apparently responsible for this quite marvellous notion. In the recipe which follows, I scoop out the savoury potato and fry it until it resembles a kind of 'rösti'. However, you can also serve it directly from inside the bird as is, spooned out into a heated serving dish.

I adore Brussels sprouts with all roasted poultry. I know that many of you will be shouting 'garden peas with roast duck please!' – and I too enjoy peas with a duck, especially very fine-quality tinned ones from France (please don't titter, they are one of my particular fads). However, I wanted some texture amongst the garnishes, so sprouts it is. Finally, I find it very difficult indeed to enjoy a roast duck without home-made apple sauce. My mother's recipe: cooking apples, sugar, water, cloves, stewed to a mush and always served cold.

The dessert which finally brings the curtain down on this sumptuous feast is, happily, a brand-new recipe. Although it is loosely based upon the original filling for a Bakewell pudding, the result is mine own. I know the word 'soufflé' is included in the title of the dish, but the technique is quietly employed rather than the raison d'être. Although it needs a deft touch when finally mixing the ingredients together, the result is both delicious – and even a little glamorous, if I may say.

Champagne cocktail

1 BOTTLE OF CHAMPAGNE WILL MAKE 5 COCKTAILS

5 white sugar cubes
15 drops Angostura bitters, 3 per sugar cube
5–6 ice cubes per glass (almost the most important part of the drink, see introduction)
100ml triple sec (or Cointreau, if you like it), 20ml per glass
100ml decent cognac (Remy Martin or Courvoisier, say), 20ml per glass
1 bottle of champagne, 150ml per glass
5 thin slices of orange

Take five roomy stemmed glasses; a finely made large tulip-shaped red wine glass might be appropriate here. Pop a sugar cube into each glass and shake the drops of Angostura over each one. Divide the ice between the glasses and pour over the triple sec and cognac. Now pour in the champagne. Carefully does it; be skimpy with the initial pour, then return to the first glass and top each one up until the champagne is evenly distributed. Slide a slice of orange into each glass and then stir with a long thin spoon to distribute all the components. Drink with great joy!

Cheese gougères

MAKES 30, OR THEREABOUTS

NOTE: AN ELECTRIC HAND WHISK IS ALMOST ESSENTIAL HERE, UNLESS YOU HAVE VERY STRONG WRISTS!

250ml water
80g butter
1 tsp sea salt
150g plain flour, sifted
4 eggs
150g grated Gruyère (the better quality the cheese, the more delicious the gougères)
⅓ nutmeg, grated
freshly ground white pepper

Preheat the oven to 200°C/gas mark 6.

•

Boil together the water, butter and salt in a roomy pan. Remove from the heat and tip in the flour all in one go. Whisk together until fully blended and the mixture is almost coming away from the sides of the pan in a ball. Leave the mixture for 3–4 minutes to cool just a little, then add the first egg and whisk it in thoroughly. Add the remaining three eggs one by one, repeating the process. Tip in the cheese, nutmeg and pepper and, once again, whisk to blend; the cheese may not become fully smooth, but this is just fine.

•

Line a flat baking tray with baking parchment; smear a tiny bit of the gougère mixture on each corner of the tray before attaching the parchment, so keeping the parchment flat. Using two dessertspoons first immersed in a bowl of hot water, mould a spoonful of mixture until as smooth as possible on all surfaces; it should resemble a smooth walnut in both shape and size. Drop each one on to the baking tray leaving at least 6cm between each one, so leaving space for the gougères to rise (it is sensible to use only half the mixture for the first baking, then cook the rest as another batch). Bake for 20–25 minutes, or until golden and verging on light brown, well puffed and light to the touch when lifted from the tray; if undercooked, they will deflate on cooling. Lift the gougères on to a cooling rack, then repeat with the remaining mixture.

•

To serve all the gougères warm, simply return them to the switched-off oven for a few minutes, leaving the door ajar.

Beetroot jelly
with fresh horseradish cream

500ml good-quality, fresh beef stock
500ml water
250ml port
650–750g raw beetroot, peeled and chopped into chunks
2 carrots, peeled and chopped into chunks
1 large leek, trimmed, thickly sliced and washed
2 cloves of garlic, chopped
1 tsp sea salt
½ tsp celery salt
1 tsp black peppercorns
1 bay leaf
4 cloves
1 level tbsp sugar

TO FINISH AND SERVE THE JELLY:

4 egg whites
500g lean beef mince
250g ready-cooked and peeled beetroot, cut into chunks (choose beetroot that is untouched by vinegar, otherwise cook your own)
3 leaves of gelatine, soaked in cold water until soft
3–4 tbsp Horseradish Cream (see below)
snipped chives

FOR THE HORSERADISH CREAM:

75g piece of fresh horseradish root, peeled and finely grated
2 tsp caster sugar
150ml soured cream
1 tbsp double cream
1 leaf of gelatine, soaked in cold water until soft

Begin by making the horseradish cream. Tip the grated horseradish into the bowl of a small food processor. Add the sugar and soured cream then process until the horseradish has blended with

the soured cream and become a touch smoother; a minute or so. Put into the fridge and leave to infuse for 30 minutes. Place a fine sieve over a bowl and tip the mixture out of the processor bowl into it. Take a small ladle and force the creamy liquid from the horseradish mulch through the sieve to end up with a completely smooth horseradish-flavoured cream. Now stir in the double cream. Put the soaked gelatine into a small pan and add a tablespoon of water. Over a very low heat, allow the gelatine to melt into the water, then scrape every last bit of this into the horseradish cream and quickly whisk in. Pour into a small plastic lidded pot and put in the fridge to set. When you wish to use the cream, give it a brief whisk, which will transform it into a kind of pouring 'sauce'.

•

Now, pour the stock, water and port into a roomy, deep pan and put on to a low heat. Place the beetroot, carrots, leek and garlic into the bowl of a food processor and pulse all together until quite finely chopped. Tip into the warming stock and water and stir together. Add the salt, celery salt, peppercorns, bay, cloves and sugar and also stir them in. Simmer all of this gently for 1 hour, covered, stirring occasionally. Strain the mixture into a clean pan through a colander and leave to drip for a good 5 minutes, then leave to become completely cold; you should now have a ruby-red broth.

•

In a large bowl, beat the egg whites until almost stiff, then tip in the beef mince and slowly mix into the egg whites until loosely blended together. Carefully tip this into the cold beetroot broth and slowly mix in thoroughly; I use my hand to do all this. Now place the pan over a moderate heat and slowly begin to bring the broth up to a simmer, stirring regularly, for about 5 minutes. Now leave this mess – it does look quite unpleasant – to gently find its own level and slowly rise to the top

of the broth as a kind of dirty raft. Once again, take this process very slowly. In several minutes you will see the broth start to push up through the beef 'raft' in several places; it is this mixture of albumen in both the egg whites *and* the raw beef that will, eventually, catch the impurities in the broth as they rise and produce a crystal-clear, ruby jellied consommé below. Now leave the broth to putter away for about 30–40 minutes. Meanwhile, take the cooked beetroot and grate it into a large bowl. Add the softened gelatine leaves to this, stir them in and put the bowl to one side.

•

Once the beetroot broth is looking clear beneath the raft, remove from the heat. Line a sieve with muslin (or a thin but clean old tea towel) and place it over the bowl with the grated beetroot beneath. Now, carefully push a portion of the raft aside and, using a ladle, decant the clear ruby broth through the muslin. Continue with this until there is none left; even tilt the pan to get to the very last spoonful.

•

Once all the broth has passed through the muslin-lined sieve, remove the sieve and discard the exhausted beetroot mulch. Now, lazily mingle the grated cooked beetroot into the clear broth with a spoon and allow to infuse together until cool. Finally – whew! – simply pass this through a sieve into something as practical as a Tupperware container that can then have its lid attached and popped into the fridge to become perfectly cool and jellied as the good lord of gastronomy intended.

•

To serve, first chill four (preferably glass) bowls in the freezer for a few minutes. Loosen the jelly a little with a metal spoon until wobbling and lovely, then ladle out four servings. Top each one with about a tablespoon of the horseradish cream then sprinkle over some snipped chives. Very good indeed eaten with thinly sliced, buttered rye bread.

Smoked cod's roe on toast with devilled eggs

SERVES 4

FOR THE DEVILLED EGGS:

4 eggs
½ tsp celery salt
½ tsp curry powder
3–4 shakes of green Tabasco sauce, or to taste
1 tbsp soured cream
2 tsp chopped dill

TO SERVE:

4 thin slices of baguette, toasted and buttered
thin slices of skinned smoked cod's roe, approx. 75–100g
freshly ground black pepper
lemon quarters
watercress, to garnish

In a small pan, cover the eggs with cold water. Bring up to a full boil then switch off the heat. Cover and leave for exactly 5 minutes, then put the pan under a cold running tap for a couple of minutes; this will stop the eggs from over-cooking. Now, carefully peel the eggs, roughly chop them and tip into a bowl. Mix with the remaining devilled egg ingredients and stir well. Spread on to the buttered toast and lay thin slices of cod's roe upon each. Grind over some black pepper and serve with lemon and watercress.

Roast duck stuffed
with potato, spring onions and sage

SERVES 4

600–650g potatoes (Maris Piper, preferably), well scrubbed but unpeeled
a thick slice of soft butter
50g trimmed spring onions, chopped
4–5 sprigs of sage, leaves chopped
1 x 2kg oven-ready Aylesbury duck, with giblets
1 level tbsp plain flour
100ml Amontillado sherry
400ml duck (or chicken) stock
salt and freshly ground white pepper

Preheat the oven to 220°C/gas mark 7.

•

Put the potatoes in a steamer and cook until only just tender; still a little bit firm in the centre is about right here. Remove from the steamer and leave to cool until you can handle them but they are still warm. Peel off the skins and then roughly mash in a wide pan with a manual masher; they need to be a bit lumpy. Stir in the butter, spring onions and sage, then lightly season and leave to cool.

•

Once cool, pack the potatoes inside the duck's cavity until completely full; while the duck is roasting, some of the potato will ooze out of the duck, browning as it so does, but this will possibly be the best bit! Place the duck on a rack inside a deep roasting tin, breast-side uppermost and slide into the oven. Roast for 20 minutes, then remove and pour off any rendered fat into a bowl. Roast for a further 20 minutes and repeat the process. During this second 20 minutes, roughly chop up

the giblets. Once the second lot of fat has been decanted, tip the chopped giblets into the roasting tin and replace the duck above them.

•

Now, turn the oven down to 190°C/gas mark 5 and continue roasting the duck for a further 30–40 minutes, or until the skin is crisp and some of the potato has oozed out into the tin. Carefully lift the duck from the tin on its rack and place on another clean oven tray, taking care to put any bits of escaped potato with it, too. Tip out all remaining fat into the bowl, bar a couple of tablespoons or so, while also taking care to leave the giblet bits behind. Allow the duck to rest on top of the stove, loosely covered in foil. Leave the oven on.

•

Put the giblet roasting tin directly over a low heat and stir in the flour. Allow to become browned with the giblets and fat – about 5 minutes – then pour in the sherry and stock and stir in. As it lightly thickens, make sure that you also scrape up any bits of giblet clinging to the tin. Allow to

simmer quietly for about 20 minutes then strain through a fine sieve into a clean saucepan. Discard the exhausted giblets. Pop the duck gravy on to a very low flame and allow to bubble quietly; as any scum or fat comes to the surface, remove it with a spoon.

•

Now, carefully remove the legs and breasts from the duck's carcass using a sharp knife, keeping it close to the carcass as you work. Return these to the roasting tin. Now scoop out all the potato from inside the carcass into a non-stick frying pan. Place this on a medium heat and spread out the potato with a spatula. Slowly begin to fry the potato mixture, while also turning it over and around in the pan; think bubble and squeak.

•

While this is going on, cook the sprouts (see overleaf) and also return the duck joints to the top of the oven and reheat for about 10 minutes, or until the duck skin has become nice and crisp; you may flash them under a moderate grill, if you like, to aid final crisping. Once the potato has become golden brown all over, slide on to a hot plate.

•

Finally present the duck joints on a heated platter and hand the potato, gravy, apple sauce and sprouts at table (recipes overleaf).

Buttered Brussels sprouts

SERVES 4

600g Brussels sprouts, trimmed and the cores criss-crossed with a sharp knife
50g butter
plenty of black pepper

Boil the sprouts in well-salted water until tender (I don't like crunchy!); eat one to check. Drain, tip back into the pan and add the butter and pepper. Toss well and then pile into a heated serving dish.

Apple sauce

SERVES 4

2 Bramley apples, peeled, cored and roughly chopped
4 cloves
2 tbsp caster sugar

Place the apples in a small stainless-steel pan, add 4–5 tablespoons of water, the cloves and sugar and stir together. Place the pan over a medium heat and, once the mixture is beginning to bubble, allow to cook very slowly, stirring occasionally, until the apples have broken down and are fully soft. Whisk together a bit to smooth the sauce slightly, then tip into a bowl and allow to cool before serving.

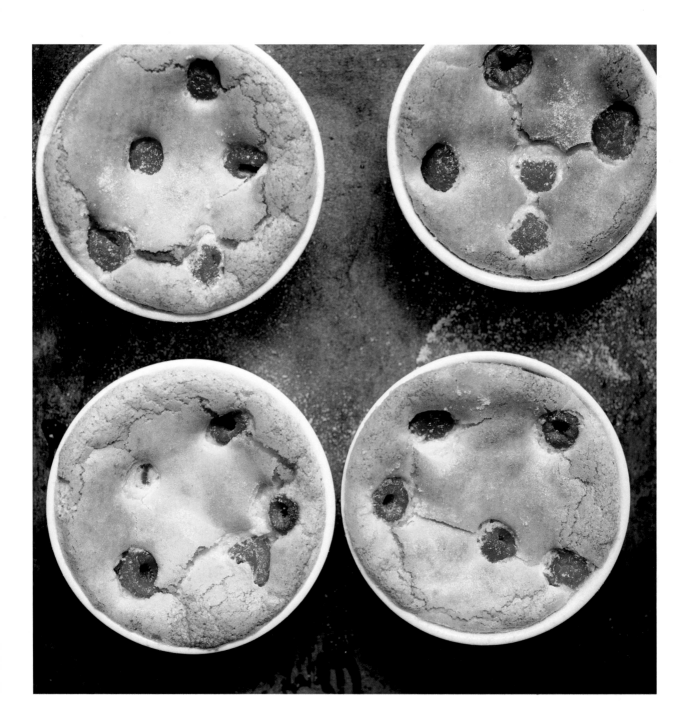

Baked almond and raspberry soufflé puddings

SERVES 4

NOTE: YOU WILL NEED FOUR 250ML RAMEKINS.

4 eggs, 3 separated
100g caster sugar, plus extra for the ramekins
100g unsalted butter, plus extra for the ramekins
pinch of salt
1 tbsp cognac
a few drops of almond essence
100g ground almonds
a little extra butter and caster sugar for lining the moulds
250g fresh raspberries
thick cream, to serve

Preheat the oven to 180°C/gas mark 4.

•

Using an electric beater, whisk together one whole egg and three yolks with 65g of the sugar until light and fluffy. Melt the butter. Whisk the three egg whites with the salt until fluffy, then gradually add the remaining sugar in a stream, whisking all the while, until a soft meringue is achieved.

•

Whisk the melted butter into the egg yolk mixture, together with the cognac and essence, then slowly mix into the meringue. Now, carefully fold in the ground almonds. Lightly butter four large ramekins (250ml capacity) and sprinkle the insides with caster sugar, tapping out any excess.

Divide half the raspberries between the four pots making a single layer over the bottom of each one. Carefully spoon the almond mixture over the raspberries – while also making sure that each pot has an equal amount of the mixture – and then deftly drop the remaining raspberries over the surface of each one; ideally, five in each pot for the prettiest appearance. Sprinkle ramekins with a touch more sugar, then bake in the oven for about 25–30 minutes, or until the puddings are nicely puffed up, springy to the touch and the surfaces are shiny and crisp. Leave to cool for a few minutes before eating with very cold, thick cream.

A celebratory dinner

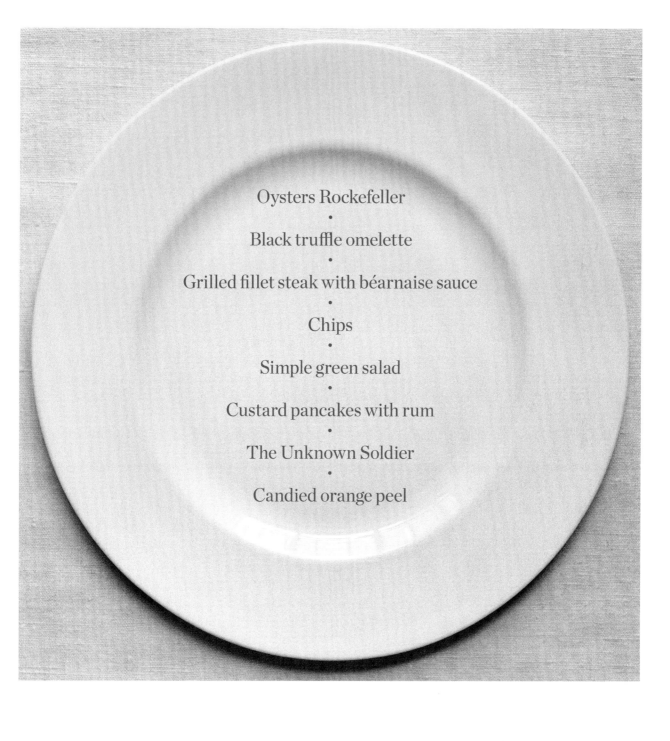

Oysters Rockefeller
·
Black truffle omelette
·
Grilled fillet steak with béarnaise sauce
·
Chips
·
Simple green salad
·
Custard pancakes with rum
·
The Unknown Soldier
·
Candied orange peel

Menu introduction

Originally, this menu's working title was to be 'All the things I love'. Well, it remains so. However, it is also celebratory, as oysters, truffles, fillet steak and béarnaise sauce are all cause for celebration, are they not? And to finish, some gorgeous pancakes and a quietly bonkers after-dinner drink that catches fire... Cake and candles? Not necessary.

Oysters Rockefeller is the best hot oyster dish I know. Period. It is unusual for me to be so manifestly positive about that which is often asked: 'What is the best...?'. Here, for once, I feel quite safe with this pesky question, as no other cooked oyster recipe comes close to this one.

Why oysters Rockefeller is quite so good lies in the perfectly chosen ingredients, which marry so well with the unique taste of an oyster. The transformation from the natural, raw oyster (delicious in itself, of course) to the warmed oyster (never too hot) is critical. Buttery creamed spinach, tarragon, parsley, the essential pastis (Pernod, here) and softened shallot and celery. The aniseed flavours have always been key; pastis added to creamed spinach, for instance, absolutely makes that particular dish sing out loud – this advice once given to me many years ago by a New York chef of my acquaintance.

A fresh black truffle is extraordinary. Both its scent and its flavour are unique but these truffles are now more rare than they have ever been in my lifetime and, sadly, more expensive because of that, too. Nevertheless, a treat is a treat, so be generous with this dark little tuber when you decide to splash out, even if it may only be once or twice during its brief appearance between late December and mid March.

It has long been understood quite how superbly the rare and costly marry so well with kitchen staples. I hesitate to refer to potatoes, rice and pasta as mundane because they are quite delicious in themselves when carefully prepared, but caviar with a baked potato, butter and soured cream is a truly wonderful thing. Truffles (particularly the even *more* ridiculously priced white truffle) are just exquisite when judiciously combined with pasta or rice; the luxe and the lowly so lovely together. However, to introduce a truffle to an everyday egg is, how shall we say, the most intriguing engagement of all.

Whenever I cook eggs and truffles, I first store the eggs in a well-sealed Tupperware-type container together with a truffle or two, carefully packaged between folds of kitchen paper; this helps to prevent the eggs accidentally cracking when jostled. As an eggshell is porous, this storage allows the scent of the truffle to powerfully invade the egg itself. And so much so that I have occasionally made a deliciously 'truffled' omelette, even when the truffle has been used up and only scented eggs remain in the container. Forty-eight hours' 'infusion' should do it, but I have been known to leave them for longer – up to five days even, especially when the truffles are super fresh.

I wish you much success with omelette-making. However, if it is something new to you, feel free to use a small, non-stick frying pan (rather than an ordinary one), which will aid the novice. And furthermore, if the very idea of omelette-making fills you with terror, you could always make two small servings of buttery scrambled eggs, served with toast 'soldiers', then simply shave some thin slices of truffle over the eggs.

I have always loved cooking and eating a fillet steak. Oh, I know that so-called 'steak experts' will pontificate over its lack of 'flavour' and that it is only about how 'tender' it is. Yes, correct! Full marks! Does this make it a poor steak? Well, no it does not. Admittedly, it may be the most expensive cut of prime beef, so only have it as an occasional treat, but it is exactly that buttery, almost fudge-like texture that appeals to me, together with its gentle, quiet flavour. For instance, a small fillet steak (the French description of *mignon* – dainty – comes to mind), simply seasoned and fried in the finest butter, is a beautiful, subtle thing. *All* cuts of good, well-hung beef steaks are delicious for different reasons – and in my view, none is in any way 'better' than the other.

And what could be more fitting with this gorgeous grilled fillet than a generous pot of béarnaise sauce? And chips. And a green salad. It is not rocket science to realise why these garnishes so perfectly complement grilled meat: a well-crusted slab of meat oozing bloody juices; a rich, piquant, buttery sauce; crisp chips; simply dressed leaves. However, if really pushed to admit, it is a chip dipped into béarnaise (and then another, and another...) that is always my initial indulgence when presented with this staggeringly good plate of food.

The custard pancakes that close this indulgent feast are loosely based upon those served at Harry's Bar in Venice. (The pancake batter here is, in fact, exactly the one used there, I have only recently begun using it, replacing an older recipe of mine, since discarded.) It may take just a little time to perfect the sugar-crusting of the pancakes but, once mastered, these gorgeous little custard-filled pillows will, I predict, become a firm favourite in gourmet kitchens up and down the land!

Shortly before I embarked upon making the television show *Simon Hopkinson Cooks*, I happened to be reading a battered old copy of a Graham Kerr cookbook (the 1970s television cook, The Galloping Gourmet), first published in 1971. At the back of the book is the drink he calls 'The Unknown Soldier'. I had forgotten all about it, but remembered making this drink for chums in my youth. It is a clever and unusual concoction and, to use a dated expression, a bit of a 'party piece'. I couldn't not include it. The recipe given is now my description, but here are some quotes from the original:

As the melting sugar hits the liquid, it causes '*small explosions...*' which sound '*...like a distant rifle*'. And it is true, they absolutely do! Also, once the flame has been extinguished, the '*Little "bullets" of caramelised sugar...*' have further turned the drink a '*...deep caramel colour...*' and with '*...an aroma of burnt orange.*'

It is suggested that the drink is consumed 'while it is still hot!' Some 40 years on, Health and Safety may well not agree with Mr Kerr. Anyway, have a glance at the recipe and all will be revealed. It will also become quite clear as to why sweet little strips of candied orange peel are a most suitable accompaniment...

Oysters Rockefeller

SERVES 2

12 rock oysters, shucked

FOR THE ROCKEFELLER PURÉE:
250g young spinach leaves
10g parsley leaves
100g unsalted butter, softened
1 large stick of celery, peeled and chopped
1 small shallot, chopped
20ml Pernod
the leaves from 3–4 sprigs of tarragon
several shakes of Tabasco sauce
¼ tsp salt
a handful of fresh breadcrumbs

Fill a pan with water and bring to the boil. Plunge in the spinach and parsley, bring back to the boil then drain in a colander. Immediately refresh in iced water until cold. Squeeze as dry as possible between two hands until no more liquid seeps out. Set aside.

•

Melt 25g of the butter in a small frying pan, gently fry the celery and shallot until softened then add the Pernod, allowing it to bubble a little. Cool briefly, then scrape into the bowl of a small food processor. Add the cooked spinach and parsley, tarragon, Tabasco, salt and the remaining 75g of butter. Purée until very smooth and set aside.

Preheat the oven to 220°C/gas mark 7.

•

Tip off any excess juice from the opened oysters and, using a small palette knife, completely cover each oyster with a generous coating of the spinach purée. Strew a baking dish (or deep metal pan) with coarse salt, to allow the oysters to sit neatly. Distribute a fine showering of breadcrumbs over the oysters and bake in the oven on the top shelf. Cook for 8–10 minutes or until the breadcrumbs have become slightly toasted. Serve without delay.

Black truffle omelette

SERVES 2

NOTE: ALWAYS HAVE A WARMED PLATE READY BY THE STOVE ON WHICH TO TIP THE OMELETTE.

4 eggs, preferably infused with a small truffle for 2–3 days
(see page 102)
butter
salt and pepper

Beat two eggs (for one omelette) together in a roomy bowl. Using a potato peeler (or truffle slicer if you happen to have one), peel away thin slices of truffle directly into the eggs – as much, or as little as you can afford – and stir in. The longer you leave them in the eggs, the more strongly they will impart flavour; 5 minutes should do it or leave them as long as 30.

Now take a favourite omelette pan and in it melt about a teaspoon of butter. Allow the butter to melt until just sizzling. Lightly season the truffled eggs and add to the pan. Once the edges of the omelette are puffing up, draw in the cooked edges to the middle, while also allowing the runny part to fill the gaps by tilting the pan a little. Continue in this fashion until the surface of the omelette remains just a little runny; this should take no longer than 45 seconds–1 minute. Now tilt up the pan and, using a palette knife, deftly fold the omelette away from you so that it rolls up in one go, then tip it straight on to the plate. Loosely cover with foil and then quickly make the second omelette.

Grilled fillet steak
with béarnaise sauce

SERVES 2

NOTE: THE BÉARNAISE REDUCTION WILL MAKE MUCH MORE THAN YOU NEED, BUT WILL KEEP
FOR MONTHS IN THE FRIDGE.

2 x 200g fillet steaks
a little olive oil
salt and pepper

FOR THE BÉARNAISE REDUCTION:
300ml tarragon vinegar
3 large or 6 small shallots, chopped
2 tbsp dried tarragon
½ tbsp coarsely crushed black peppercorns

FOR THE BÉARNAISE SAUCE:
3 egg yolks
200g unsalted butter, melted
lemon juice (optional)
the leaves from 3–4 sprigs of tarragon, finely chopped
a little salt and pepper

To make the béarnaise reduction, put all the ingredients into a stainless-steel saucepan and bring up to a boil. Reduce to a low simmer and cook, uncovered, until the mixture has reduced by about three quarters; about 30 minutes. (Note: have the extraction on full whack, as the reduction is very strong.)

•

Suspend a fine sieve over a bowl and pour the mixture into it. Using a small ladle, press down on all the tarragon/shallot mixture until no more liquid emerges below. Decant into a small bottle or jar and keep in the fridge until needed.

To make the béarnaise sauce, whisk the egg yolks in a stainless-steel pan (preferably with rounded contours in the base of the pan, where the whisk won't miss any egg yolk) with a splash of water, over a low heat, until thick and smooth. Off the heat, continue to whisk while pouring in the melted butter (remove any surface scum) in a thin stream, leaving behind the milky residue that has settled in the bottom of the butter pan.

•

Once the sauce is wobbly and glossy, add dribbles of the béarnaise reduction to the sauce until well flavoured, but not too vinegary; a scant tablespoon,

say. Sharpen with lemon juice if you think it needs it, stir in the tarragon and season. Decant into a serving bowl and keep warm over a pan of hot – not boiling – water while you grill the steaks.

Season the steaks, brush with olive oil and cook on a ribbed, stove-top grill until done to your liking. Serve with the béarnaise sauce, chips and a simple green salad (recipes overleaf).

Chips

SERVES 2

oil (vegetable or peanut, for instance), for deep-frying
2 large Maris Piper potatoes, peeled, cut into chips,
well washed in cold water, drained and dried
fine salt

Heat the oil to 140°C. Put the potatoes into the frying basket and carefully lower them into the oil. Fry for about 7–8 minutes, lift them out and pinch one to see if they are soft. At this stage, you do not want them to colour; if you notice that they are turning a touch golden, turn the temperature down a little. Now tip these floppy chips out on to a paper-lined tray and leave to cool; you may do this a few hours in advance, keeping the chips covered, in the fridge.

To finish the chips, turn the frying temperature up to full; on most machines, this is around about 180°C (I actually think you need 190°C, for the most crisp of chips, so search around for a deep-fryer that has this higher temperature). Return the chips to the oil and fry again for 1–2 minutes, or until they are crisp and golden. Sprinkle with fine salt and serve at once.

Simple green salad

SERVES 2

NOTE: THIS RECIPE WILL CLEARLY MAKE MUCH MORE DRESSING THAN YOU WILL NEED FOR A SALAD FOR TWO. HOWEVER, KEEP IT IN A SCREW-TOP JAR IN THE FRIDGE, WHERE IT WILL HAPPILY KEEP FOR A WEEK OR TWO, READY TO MAKE MORE SALADS WHENEVER YOU FEEL LIKE THEM.

2 tbsp smooth Dijon mustard
2 tbsp red wine vinegar
a little lukewarm water
325ml sunflower oil
simple round lettuces in spring/summer or, if you like, lamb's lettuce (mâche) in winter
salt and pepper

To make the dressing, put the mustard, vinegar, seasoning and a couple of tablespoons of the water in a blender or food processor. Process until smooth and then start adding the oil in a thin stream. When the consistency is creamy white, have a taste. If you think it is too thick, add a little more water; the consistency should be one of thin salad cream. Now dress the salad.

Custard pancakes with rum

SERVES 2

NOTE: THIS RECIPE MAKES MORE THAN ENOUGH FOR TWO SERVINGS (AS MUCH AS SIX, IN FACT)
BUT IT IS IMPRACTICAL TO MAKE LESS.

FOR THE PANCAKE BATTER:
3 eggs
pinch of salt
100g plain flour
125ml full-fat milk and 125ml water mixed together
1 tbsp light olive oil
a little butter for the pan

FOR THE CUSTARD FILLING:
350ml full-fat milk
4 strips of lemon zest, removed with a potato peeler, taking care that no pith remains on the zest
4 egg yolks
75g golden caster sugar
1 heaped tbsp plain flour
1 tsp vanilla extract

TO FINISH THE PANCAKES:
a little beaten egg
1–2 thin slices of butter
a sprinkle or two of golden caster sugar
a good glug or two of dark rum

To make the batter, put the eggs and salt into a mixing bowl. Whisk together and then begin to introduce the flour while continuing to whisk. Once it becomes almost too difficult to work, pour in a little of the milk/water mix to thin the batter. When it is thin enough to whisk once more, add a little more flour. Continue until both liquid and flour are used up. Whisk in the oil and put to one side for at least 30 minutes; the batter may be made up to 6 hours in advance if you want to get ahead.

For the pancakes, use a 20cm frying pan (non-stick if you are a novice at pancake making) and in it melt a tiny amount of butter. Allow it to become hot and sizzling, then lazily wipe out the pan with a piece of kitchen paper but leaving a thin sheen of butter behind. Now, pour in enough batter to thinly cover the base of the pan; when it is turning golden at the edges, flip it over with a palette knife and cook the other side for about 30 seconds. Continue in this mode for subsequent pancakes;

you may happily stack them together on a plate, once finished. And don't worry, they won't stick together.

•

To make the custard filling, warm the milk in a pan with the strips of lemon zest. Once the milk is scalded (heated until it hasn't quite reached a boil), put on a lid and leave to infuse. Put the egg yolks into a bowl and whisk together with the caster sugar until well blended and pale coloured. Add the flour and beat this in too. Now, strain the lemon-scented milk over this (don't wash the pan) and whisk all together until smooth. Add the vanilla extract and return to the pan (don't wash the bowl, either) and heat over a very low flame, stirring constantly with a wooden spoon, until it slowly begins to thicken.

•

Alternate, now, between the spoon and a sturdy whisk, as the custard will soon begin to thicken dramatically; the difference between a simple egg custard and this one (essentially the thick French custard known as 'crème patissière') is that the addition of flour will stabilise the mixture as it cooks and, unusually, one can actually allow it to enjoy the occasional simmering blip as it thickens, without worrying about the egg scrambling. And it *must* eventually thicken to something resembling the consistency of a thick white sauce. Once this has been achieved, take a spatula and scrape out the custard back into the bowl. Lay a sheet of clingfilm directly over the surface of the custard (this prevents a skin forming) and allow to cool.

To assemble and finish the custard pancakes, take one pancake, lay it on a work surface and then brush a little beaten egg over the top edge furthest away from you. Now place a tablespoon of the custard in the centre of the pancake, roll up the pancake halfway to cover it, then tuck in the sides and finish rolling up to seal; it will resemble a plump spring roll. Make three more of these. Note: do not roll them too tightly.

•

Melt a little butter in a non-stick frying pan large enough to easily accommodate four custard pancakes, and allow it to gently heat. Now lay in the pancakes, sealed-side down, and leave to sizzle quietly for about 30 seconds. Using a palette knife, deftly flip them over. Sprinkle with a tiny amount of sugar, then flip them over once more. Sprinkle with more sugar on this buttery side, then flip over again. Repeat this process once more; the time taken should be about 5 minutes, during which time the pancakes will have puffed and swelled somewhat (the reason for not rolling up the pancakes too tightly) and become lightly crusted with sugar.

•

Remove the pancakes to a warmed serving dish. Add a touch more sugar to the pan, now over a slightly higher heat, together with a scrap of butter. Let them sizzle a bit, then add two healthy glugs of rum and let the mixture bubble and amalgamate into what resembles a modicum of butterscotch sauce. Quickly pour this over the pancakes and serve without delay.

The Unknown Soldier

MAKES 2 DRINKS

NOTE: YOU WILL NEED TWO FORKS, TWO 50ML LIQUEUR GLASSES AND ONE MATCH.

50ml vodka
50ml Cointreau
2 small white sugar lumps

Pour the vodka and Cointreau into two glasses that have previously been heated with boiling water; this will help the alcohols to ignite. Dim the room lights and silence any guests. Have ready one lump of sugar balanced on the tines of a fork, then light the first drink with a match. Suspend the fork over the flame and allow the sugar lump to melt and drip into the drink below. This is the really special moment (see introduction). Leave to cool a little before drinking...

Candied orange peel

MAKES ABOUT 80–100 ORANGE STRIPS

1kg best-quality oranges (4–5, depending on size)
400g golden caster sugar

Cut off each end of the oranges to reveal the flesh. Cut oranges in half lengthways, and then each half into thirds, then cut these in two lengthways to give six segments per half orange. Using a small, sharp serrated knife, cut off two thirds of the flesh from each segment with respect to the shape of it; in other words, curve the knife as you cut, while also leaving one third of the orange's flesh attached to the peel. Put the pure flesh segments into a plastic container, cover and keep in the fridge to eat for breakfast the next day.

•

Now, cut each segment lengthways into four equal strips and put into a stainless-steel pan. Cover with cold water and bring up to a simmer. Cook for 5 minutes, then drain in a colander. Return to the pan, cover again with water and repeat the previous process. Do this twice more. Once the strips have been cooked and drained **four times** (this repetition is absolutely necessary, to rid excess bitter taste from the orange's pith), return to the pan and add 300g of the sugar and gently stir together; do **not** add any water. Over a low heat, allow the sugar to dissolve among the orange strips and then allow to bubble away very, very gently for about an hour, gently stirring occasionally. What will happen here, is that any moisture from the oranges will evaporate while the sugar reduces to a thick syrup; in effect, the syrup will be absorbed into the peel until there is very little left to see. At this point, they are ready.

•

Tip the now very sticky orange peel on to a cake-cooling rack (slide a tray or sheet of foil underneath to catch drips) to cool slightly for a few minutes; don't allow them to become stone cold or they will all stick together! Now, fill a shallow tray with the remaining 100g of sugar, pick off the orange strips and roll them in the sugar until each one is well coated; if you need to add more sugar to make sure of this, feel free. The finished candied orange peel is best served cold from the fridge.

A CELEBRATORY DINNER

121

A summer lunch

Bloody Mary

Celery nibbles

Pork rillettes

A warm salad of leeks, brown shrimps & dill

Poached salmon with cucumber, chives & cream

Buttered new potatoes

Watercress salad

Basil ice cream

Menu introduction

I cannot think of many things I enjoy more than a summer lunch eaten out of doors, with the sun shining and an enormous brolly to shade it from the table – and from me, most particularly. Those that ill-advisedly choose to sit in direct sunlight must be mad. And, furthermore, the butter melts, the salad limps, the glass of crisp, cool rosé warms up...

Good drinks are most important, naturally, and I can think of no finer way to begin this particular lunch than with a well-made Bloody Mary. The negatives first. I do not like a Bloody Mary drowned by tomato juice, and it also shouldn't be thick and viscous from the wrong type of juice; this is a drink, not a soup. Although I adore fresh horseradish, it is inappropriate here, especially when bits of the grated root get stuck in your teeth with every single sip. A thick stick of celery – especially when not peeled of its stringy skin – simply gets in the way when one tries to drink, and if you want to take it out, where the dickens do you put it? And those bartenders who think it is nice (clever?) to dip the dampened rim of the glass in celery salt – rather than mixing it into the drink – should seek help as soon as possible.

The positives: the tomato juice should be the best you can find/afford; you *must* be able to taste the vodka and sherry; there should be plenty of ice to keep the drink cold till the last drop. Let us be quite clear: a Bloody Mary is, quite simply, one of the very best reviving midday drinks on a summer's day.

The celery, cream cheese and jalapeño nibbles are a sensible and delicious way to partner a Bloody Mary. The cool and creamy cheese spiked by the fresh zing of chilli marries really well with the drink. And by the way, the Bloody Mary was, by all accounts, created by a bartender working at Harry's American Bar at 5 rue Daunou, Paris, in the early 1920s. American visitors to the City of Light over the decades since, keen to find this legendary bar (Hemingway was a regular) would, helpfully, be given a written note with its address: 'sank-roo-doe-noo'.

There is something very comforting about eating rillettes of any kind, be they made from duck, goose, or, occasionally, rabbit. However, for me, the finest remains that which are made from pork – and good, fatty belly pork with a good pedigree, in particular. Spread thickly upon some especially good, crusty baguette, together with perky cornichons to cut the richness, this absolutely French potted pork is everything that defines that country's gastronomic tradition.

The following recipe is based upon one given by Elizabeth David in her seminal work *French Provincial Cooking* (Michael Joseph, 1960). It is simple to prepare, with time only expended curing the meat, together with the gentle heat of an oven to cook it. This quietly made dish will repel only the impatient cook who wishes for a dish to be ready in 15 minutes. For others who enjoy a day or two preparing something so very worthwhile, patience can only be a pleasure.

The delectable and, dare I say, diminutive warm collation of leeks and shrimps was a late addition to this menu. Quite often when planning a lunch for friends, I have all sorts of ideas up my sleeve and it can take me a day or so to finally decide upon what I am going to cook. I always knew that I wanted to use some delicious brown shrimps; so easy to use, presented ready-peeled and packed in small plastic boxes, and with a good fridge life, too. Dill is a perfect herb, here, evoking Scandinavian flavours in the tiny, comma-like shellfish, simply dressed with lemon juice and some fine olive oil. The vinegar, too, with the leeks reminds me of one of my most favourite French vegetable dishes: leeks vinaigrette.

In recent years I have discovered that an excellent thickener of chilled sauces can be achieved simply by adding gelatine to them (as a fine example of this, I use this gelatine idea to very good effect in a horseradish cream to anoint a beetroot jelly; see the Sunday Roast menu, page 77). However, here, in this most summery main dish of salmon, it is a cream-enriched, simple fish stock that is 'set' by the gelatine, allowed to chill to a firm-ish consistency, then vigorously whisked together to slacken it to a pouring consistency. Chives are added for their perfect, summery

savour and then the sauce is poured over the poached, then flaked fish. It will set once more after 30 minutes or so when returned to the fridge.

I do urge you to have a go at what may, at first glance, appear to be a complicated little number. However, it really is only a matter of making the simple stock, poaching the fish in it and adding gelatine and cream. And anyone can slice a cucumber, can't they?

And, finally, an ice cream to finish. It was in a posh Italian restaurant, about 15 years ago, that I first tasted a beautiful ice cream scented with basil. Could I guess the flavour (it was presented to me blind)? No, I could not! After much guessing and irritation, the secret ingredient was revealed to me – along with much hilarity – by my triumphant hosts. This basil ice cream is, all at once, intriguing, elusive and astonishingly good. Be brave; I never would have been, until I was converted by those who knew better. Story of my life...

Bloody Mary

MAKES 4

plenty of ice cubes
300ml tomato juice
75ml vodka
50ml dry sherry
2 tsp Worcestershire sauce
1 tsp Tabasco sauce
juice of 1 small lemon (or 1 lime)
¼ tsp celery salt
a few grindings of black pepper

Half-fill a large glass jug with ice and add all the other ingredients. Stir well and then strain into four ice-filled glasses.

Celery nibbles

SERVES 4

2 small celery hearts, outer sticks peeled
200g cream cheese
2–3 jalapeño chillies

Fill the celery with cream cheese using a small table knife and cut into short, bite-size lengths.

Deseed the jalapeños, thinly slice them and garnish each piece of celery with these, to taste.

Pork rillettes

MAKES 6 X 250ML GLASS KILNER JARS

NOTE: BEGIN THE RECIPE THE DAY BEFORE YOU WISH TO COOK IT. ALSO, ONCE MADE, I RECOMMEND ALLOWING THE RILLETTES TO 'MATURE' FOR FIVE DAYS BEFORE EATING.

1 tbsp sea salt
1 tbsp caster sugar
2 bay leaves
6 cloves
about ½ a nutmeg, grated
1 level tbsp juniper berries
2 tsp black peppercorns
1.2kg belly pork, bones and rind removed but both reserved
500g fresh pork back fat
6 large cloves of garlic, peeled and crushed
4–5 sprigs of sage, leaves removed and roughly chopped
200ml dry white wine

TO SERVE:

toasted baguette
cornichons

Using a small food processor, grind together the first seven ingredients to a fine powder. Cut the belly pork and back fat into approximately 2cm cubes. Spread out on a work surface and sprinkle with the powder. Thoroughly mix together with your hands, turning the meat and fat over and over, then add the bones and rind of the belly (left as large pieces, so they are easier to remove once cooked) into the mix. Tip into a large Tupperware container and put on the lid. Place in the fridge and leave overnight.

•

The next day, begin by preheating the oven to 140°C/gas mark 1.

Put all the meat, pork fat and bones into a solid-based pot (a Le Creuset is ideal here). Bury the garlic and sage into this mass, then pour in the wine. Mix everything together and hands, once again, are best here. Place the pot over a low heat for about 5 minutes, stirring often; this is simply to bring the assembly up to heat before it goes into the oven. Put on the lid and slide into the oven. Cook quietly for about 3 hours.

•

Remove from the oven and leave to cool for about 20 minutes. Fetch out the pork bones and rind, and discard. Suspend a colander over a large bowl and into it tip the contents of the pot. Allow to drip for about 5 minutes, then decant the liquid fat into a small bowl. Tip the long-cooked pork and fat into the large bowl and, using an electric hand mixer, briefly blend the small pieces of meat and fat into shreds. Now lift off a small ladle of pure melted fat from the small bowl and add a little at a time, while further mixing it in. Continue with 2–3 ladlefuls until you are happy with the taste and creamy texture. Note: there will be a modicum of juice beneath the fat, so tip off the fat into yet another bowl and then add this hidden juice to the pork mixture, too.

Now, pack the rillette mixture into small lidded pots or similarly-sized Kilner jars. (Please either boil the jars to sterilise, or fill to their brims with boiling water, at least, before filling.) Smooth over the surface and then spoon over the remaining pork fat to seal each one. Attach the lids and put into the fridge. Leave to mature for at least five days before eating. However, they can happily be kept for at least a further 2–3 weeks – even a month or so – without spoiling. Eat with short lengths of split baguette – toasted or grilled – and with a pot of crisp cornichons close at hand.

A warm salad of leeks, brown shrimps and dill

SERVES 4

4 large, well trimmed leeks (approx. 450g)
150g peeled brown shrimps
2–3 generous squeezes of lemon juice
several sprigs of dill, fronds removed and finely chopped
a trickle or two of fine red wine vinegar
1–2 tbsp extra virgin olive oil
salt and freshly ground black pepper

Cut each leek into 5–6 short barrels, equal in length, then place in a shallow dish on their ends. Season with a little salt and put into a steamer. Cook for about 10–15 minutes, or until tender when pierced with a small, sharp knife. Meanwhile, mix the shrimps with the lemon juice in a bowl and stir in the chopped dill.

Remove the leeks from the steamer once cooked, then put on to a handsome serving dish. Leave until lukewarm. Trickle over the vinegar and then evenly scatter the shrimps over the leeks. Spoon over the olive oil until all is nicely coated, but not drenched. Finally, grind over plenty of black pepper and serve forthwith.

Poached salmon with cucumber, chives and cream

SERVES 4

2 cucumbers
4–5 sprigs of parsley, roughly chopped
4–5 sprigs of dill, roughly chopped
1 tsp sea salt
a few peppercorns
1 thumb-size knob of fresh ginger, sliced
1 bay leaf
2 large shallots, sliced
400ml water
150ml Lillet (or dry vermouth)
100g smoked salmon offcuts, roughly chopped
500g salmon fillet
4 leaves of gelatine, soaked in cold water until soft
200ml double cream
juice of ½ small lemon
large pinch of cayenne pepper
1 small bunch of chives, finely chopped

Peel one of the cucumbers (keep the peel), chop the other into small chunks. Cut the peeled cucumber in half, deseed with a teaspoon then put the cucumber halves in a small plastic bag and keep in the fridge until later. Add the seeds to the peelings and chopped cucumber and put all of this into a stainless-steel pan. Now add the parsley, dill, salt, peppercorns, ginger, bay leaf and shallots to the pan. Cover with the water and pour in the Lillet. Bring up to a boil, then allow to simmer for 15 minutes. Stir in the smoked salmon and continue simmering for a further 10 minutes.

Place the fresh salmon in another, smaller stainless-steel pan into which the salmon fits snugly. Using a fine sieve, strain the cucumber/smoked salmon stock directly over the fresh salmon (discard the solids). Place the salmon and stock over a low heat and just bring up to a simmer. Remove from the heat, put on a lid and leave to finish cooking for 15–20 minutes. Have a poke at the fish after 15 minutes to check whether it is cooked through; it should be only *just* cooked through in the centre. Remove from the stock and put on to a plate. Once cooled a little, carefully remove any skin and unsightly brown parts. Cover with clingfilm and cool completely before putting in the fridge.

Bring the stock to a simmer, remove any unsightly scum that rises to the surface, then allow to reduce by about a quarter. Add the soaked gelatine, stir in and pour into a bowl. After about 10 minutes, stir in the cream, lemon juice and cayenne pepper. Now place in the fridge to set for at least 2 hours, or more. This, eventually, will be a sauce for the salmon.

·

Remove the reserved, peeled cucumber from the fridge and slice into little half-moon shapes. Strew these over the base of a shallow serving dish to cover it evenly, then lightly season with salt and pepper. Break up the salmon with your fingers and lay over the cucumber. Remove the 'sauce' from the fridge and whisk (an electric hand-whisk is best for this) until absolutely smooth and creamy, then briefly whisk in the chives. Carefully spoon over the salmon until fully coated. Return to the fridge until ready to serve; if possible, for at least 15 minutes or so, to give the sauce a little time to set once again. You may, of course, leave it in the fridge until you are ready to serve, but not longer than an hour or so. Buttered new potatoes and a watercress salad would go well here (see overleaf).

Buttered new potatoes

SERVES 4

16–20 new potatoes, depending upon size and appetite
a thick slice of unsalted butter
sea salt

Boil or steam the potatoes in salted water until tender. Drain and cool until warm, then peel them. Melt the butter in a frying pan, add the potatoes and warm through, while carefully coating them well with the butter. Serve forthwith.

Watercress salad

SERVES 4

4 bunches of watercress, trimmed of all tough stalks
juice of 1 lemon
2–3 tbsp extra virgin olive oil
sea salt and freshly ground black pepper

Place the watercress in a large salad bowl and, using your hands, deftly mix together with the remaining ingredients.

Basil ice cream

SERVES 4

4 large egg yolks
150g caster sugar
400ml full-fat milk
1 large pot of basil, or 3 large packets, roughly chopped
300ml double cream
raspberries (optional), to serve

Whisk the egg yolks with the caster sugar until thick and creamy. Scald the milk (heat it until it hasn't quite reached a boil) and whisk about half of it into the egg yolk/sugar mixture until smooth. Tip this back into the remaining milk in the pan and stir together. Add the basil and stir in. Slowly cook over a low flame until beginning to thicken, stirring constantly. A thermometer is useful here: the mixture will be ready when the temperature reaches 85ºC, or when the consistency is of thin custard. Remove from the heat, pour into a bowl and allow to cool slightly.

Stir in the cream and then cover with a layer of clingfilm directly over the surface of the custard (this prevents a skin forming). Leave in the fridge for at least 4 hours – or even overnight – to infuse and cool.

•

Strain through a fine sieve into a clean bowl, pressing down well on the basil leaves using a ladle, until all the custard has been forced through. Pour the basil-infused custard into an ice-cream machine and churn. Very good indeed eaten with raspberries.

A very British luncheon

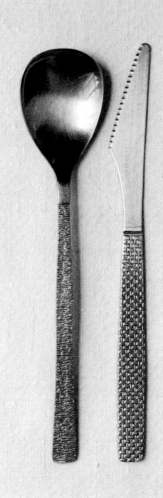

Pimm's
·
Lancashire cheese & onion biscuits
·
Cream of celery soup
·
English salad
·
Chicken pie
·
Stewed carrots & peas
·
Marmalade queen of puddings

Menu introduction

I still have an empty bottle of Pimm's No. 2 Cup which I had saved from my father's old drinks cupboard. No. 2 is 'The Original Whisky Sling', but I now slavishly decant a new bottle of what is now regarded as the only Pimm's – 'The No. 1 Cup. The Original Gin Sling' – into this venerable old bottle at the beginning of every summer. It has such a beautiful label, which always makes me smile - especially as the alcohol proof is shown as 60°! These days, the proof of Pimm's No.1 is a rather paltry 25°, which is why I always add an extra glug of neat gin when mixing up a jug.

A word of advice: although a Pimm's with the prefix 'Royal' may sound glamorous, don't be taken in. This is a Pimm's topped-up with champagne instead of the more usual, and for me, essential, lemonade. The drink really needs the added sweetness, not more alcohol in the way of wildly inappropriate fizzy wine. I guess that it is the bubbles in champagne that causes bewildered folk to think that this is a wizard wheeze. It is not. Furthermore, only one of these will swiftly take the casual imbiber to la-la land before one can say 'I think I'll have *just* another one...'.

The 'garnishes' for a perfect Pimm's Cup should be discreet. It is not a fruit salad. Rather, it is a refreshing summer drink. So... no strawberries, no apple, no raspberries, pears, pineapple, grapes... In fact, no fruit other than citrus, please. A slice or two of orange and lemon will do just fine. However, strips of cucumber peel are, for me, *essential*, as are several sprightly sprigs of mint. Borage is traditional, too – so much so, that it is a suggested addition on the label of Dad's old bottle. It is said that the herb has a whiff of cucumber about it, though I have never been able to detect this.

And, finally, the remaining four original Pimm's Cups were brandy (No. 3), vodka (No.6 – and still made), rum (No.4) and rye whiskey (No.5). It is a fun question to ask of a know-it-all bartender – to name every one. It is rumoured that there was once a No.7 – the tequila Pimm's Cup. Ah well, so there it is.

I am suggesting a plate of cheese and onion biscuits to nibble with a glass of Pimm's. These, as ever, are based upon an original recipe given to me by my friend Rachel Cooke. In this particular outing they are made from Lancashire cheese and chopped spring onions. To soak up the extra juices given up by the onion (which would otherwise sog the finished biscuits a little), I have introduced a modicum of ground almonds. Do try to find a 'tasty' Lancashire cheese, for best results.

My partner at Bibendum, Sir Terence Conran, said to me after having perused our inaugural menu in 1987: 'Don't you think that a cream of celery soup somewhat smacks of a 1950s British boarding house?'. I said no. And I still say no. The only soup of that era that was forever a poor one was the 'Brown Windsor'. Its very name does not exactly endear it – even to the most easy-going of gourmets. At the very most, this was a weak beef broth thickened with flour. Go figure.

Any creamed vegetable soup, carefully and thoughtfully made, can be one of the most delicious things it is possible to eat. Why, singularly, would one denigrate a soup made from celery? If it were a leek and potato soup, say (a *potage bonne femme* – and that's your actual French), perhaps the unwarranted criticism would have evaporated in a puff of steam from the nozzle of a Prestige pressure cooker. In the 1950s, this was *the* favoured and novel method of cooking a soup, both saving on gas and keeping nutrients active within a sealed, fiercely boiling turmoil. And today, let me tell you, a pressure cooker continues to make excellent soup.

Truthfully, however, I think that Terence's memory only saw a cream of celery soup as that which may have been made from a 'big bad catering powdered soup mix'. The recipe that I give here should, finally, convince him that I knew different.

Perhaps any association with 'salad cream' might further bring back memories of the dreaded boarding-house high tea of yore. It certainly does for me – and my prep school version was one of the very worst: undressed, limp lettuce leaves, wet tomatoes, vinegary beetroot, slimy cucumber, hard-boiled eggs with a nice grey ring surrounding the bullet-hard yolk and even cold, grey, leathery-skinned broad beans, too! What were *they* doing there? (As it is, it took me a further 10 years to finally stomach a broad bean.) The English salad

I offer here will banish all those dreadful moments and, if I may also say, the home-made accompanying salad cream is delicious.

Are not the two words 'Chicken Pie' possibly the most comforting of all in the lexicon of English cookery prose? Well, this old cook thinks they are. For me this announces golden pastry with that delicious, slightly soggy underneath, fondant nuggets of chicken in a thick cream and parsley sauce and little bits of slippery mushroom lurking here and there. What's not to love? And when partnered with a sweet and savoury dish of buttered peas and carrots, my dream centrepiece to this luncheon is complete.

To close this Albionian feast, what could be more fitting and apt than a queen of puddings.? When I made this rather good edition for the first time, it was simply that there wasn't any jam in the cupboard. But there *was* a jar of marmalade that had been given to me by a marmalade-making chum. It is not a preserve that I would ever go out of my way to buy, let alone make, but I very much enjoy the taste. Marmalade is very good indeed, here; its bitter taste gives a pleasing contrast to the rather more full-on-sweet jam that is the norm for a Q of P. The idea was given to me years ago by a friend who, would you believe, was also fresh out of jam...

Pimm's

plenty of ice
300ml Pimm's No. 1 Cup
100ml gin
750ml lemonade
8 sprigs of mint (apple mint if you can lay your hands on some; 4 sprigs for the jug, 4 for the glasses)
8 long strips of cucumber peel (4 for the jug, 4 for the glasses)
8 thin slices of orange (4 for the jug, 4 for the glasses)
8 thin slices of lemon (4 for the jug, 4 for the glasses)

Mix everything together vigorously in a large glass jug, then leave to infuse for 5 minutes. Strain the liquid into ice-filled, large glass beakers. Garnish each beaker with a mint sprig, a strip of cucumber peel and a slice of lemon and orange. Imbibe forthwith.

Lancashire cheese and onion biscuits

MAKES ABOUT 30 BISCUITS

100g plain flour
50g ground almonds
60g trimmed spring onions, roughly chopped
pinch of salt
¼ tsp cayenne pepper
½ heaped tsp mustard powder
100g cold, unsalted butter, cut into chunks
100g tasty Lancashire cheese, coarsely grated, plus a little extra, finely grated
1 egg, beaten

Place the flour, almonds and spring onions in the bowl of a food processor, together with the salt, cayenne and mustard powder. Process until the onions have become small, pale green specks amongst the dry ingredients. Add the butter and coarsely grated cheese and further process together until the mixture begins to form small, doughy lumps. Now, start to pulse the mixture in short spurts as you begin to notice everything clumping together – as with pastry, if you like. Once the texture is clearly becoming a single, coherent mass, tip out on to a lightly floured surface and deftly, but thoroughly, knead it together until well blended and smooth. Wrap in clingfilm and chill in the fridge for at least 30 minutes. Preheat the oven to 170°C/gas mark 3.

•

Lightly flour a work surface and gently roll out the pastry to about 2mm thick. Cut out the biscuits with a 5cm plain or fluted round biscuit cutter. Lay them out on to a greased baking tray about 1cm apart. Carefully brush the surface of each biscuit with the beaten egg and sprinkle over a little of the finely grated cheese. Bake in the oven for about 15–20 minutes, or until they have risen somewhat and are evenly gilded. Carefully lift them off the tray on to a cooling rack, with a palette knife. Cool for 30 minutes before serving.

Cream of celery soup

SERVES 4

50g butter
2 small onions, peeled and chopped
250g celery, cleaned and finely chopped
300g celeriac, peeled and cut into small chunks
½ tsp celery salt
1 litre tasty chicken stock
200ml whipping cream
freshly ground white pepper
buttery croutons, to serve

Melt the butter in a roomy pot and gently sweat the onions in it until softened. Add the celery, celeriac and celery salt, stir together and quietly stew for about 20 minutes, partially covered. Now add the chicken stock and bring up to a simmer; check the seasoning to see if any further salt is needed and remove any scum with a spoon. Cook for 30 minutes or until the vegetables are very soft indeed when pressed with a spoon.

Liquidise well for a minute or longer, as this will help achieve a very smooth soup. Push through a fine sieve and return to a clean pan. Stir in the cream and pepper, then gently reheat but do not boil. Serve with a bowl of buttery croutons.

English salad

SERVES 4

4 eggs
2 crisp cos lettuce hearts, trimmed of all outer, dark green leaves
4 ripe tomatoes, peeled and sliced
½ cucumber, peeled and sliced
6 spring onions, trimmed and sliced into short lengths
1 bunch radishes, trimmed, washed and quartered
4 small cooked beetroot, peeled and sliced

FOR THE SALAD CREAM (MAKES ABOUT 400ML):
150ml milk
1 tsp mustard powder
1 tsp salt
1 level tbsp caster sugar
a thin slice of butter
2 eggs, beaten
2–3 tbsp malt vinegar, to taste

To make the salad cream, first put the milk, mustard powder, salt, sugar and butter into a basin set over a saucepan of just simmering water. Whisking well, slowly incorporate the beaten eggs, then add a little of the vinegar to begin with, to taste. Continue to whisk gently, tasting as you proceed and adding more vinegar until satisfied with the flavour. The mixture will soon begin to thicken to that of the consistency of double cream, at which point the salad cream is ready. Decant into a clean bowl and allow to cool while you gather together the salad.

•

Firstly, cook the eggs. Just cover with cold water and bring up to a boil. Switch off the heat, cover, and leave in the water for exactly 4 minutes. Put the pan under a cold running tap and let it run, slowly, for at least 5 minutes, then lift out the eggs. Carefully wash the cos lettuce in very cold water, spin or shake dry and lay out on a handsome, large platter. Peel and quarter the eggs, then arrange them attractively over the lettuce together with the tomatoes, cucumber, spring onions, radishes and beetroot. Spoon over the salad cream and serve at once.

•

(Note: if you feel that the salad cream is a touch too thick, thin it with a little more milk. Also, any left over can be stored in a screw-top jar in the fridge, where it will keep well for a couple of weeks.)

Chicken pie

SERVES 4

NOTE: YOU WILL NEED A DEEP LOOSE-BOTTOMED TART TIN APPROX. 20 X 4CM.

700–750g chicken thighs, with bone
1 large onion, peeled and quartered
1 large carrot, peeled and sliced
2 sticks of celery, sliced
75ml white wine
1 chicken stock cube
1 bay leaf
25g butter
2 large leeks, trimmed of almost all green parts, thickly sliced, then washed
150g medium white mushrooms, sliced
1 tbsp plain flour
2 tbsp chopped parsley
plenty of freshly ground white pepper
100ml double cream

FOR THE PASTRY:
75g cold unsalted butter, cubed
75g cold lard, cubed, plus a little extra for greasing the tart tin
250g plain flour
large pinch of salt
iced water, to mix
1 egg, beaten and mixed with a little milk, to glaze

To make the pastry, place the butter and lard in a bowl with the flour and salt or place all four in the bowl of a food processor. Gently rub the fat into the flour using fingertips until the texture resembles very coarse breadcrumbs or pulse to a breadcrumb-like texture then transfer to a clean bowl. Add 2–3 tablespoonfuls of the iced water and stir together with a knife. Once the mixture begins to come together, tip out on to a work surface and gently knead until well blended. Form into a thick disk and put it in the fridge for at least 30 minutes, to rest and firm up.

•

Put the chicken thighs into a roomy pot and add the onion, carrot, celery, wine, stock cube and bay. Just cover with cold water and place over a moderate heat. Bring up to a simmer and skim off any scum that rises to the surface. Cook very gently for about 40 minutes, continuing to skim if necessary.

Lift out the thighs using a slotted spoon, while flicking off any clinging bits of vegetable, then put on to a plate to cool for a few minutes before removing the skin and discarding it. Now, strain the broth through a fine sieve into a large, clean saucepan and discard the debris. Allow the broth to settle for a few minutes, then remove any surface fat with kitchen paper. Place over a moderate heat again and reduce by about half its volume (more scum will be generated, so remove it as and when). Using your fingers, break up the chicken thigh meat into small pieces, throw away the bones and put the meat into a bowl.

•

Preheat the oven to 200°C/gas mark 6. Also, place a flat baking sheet on the middle shelf.

•

Rinse out the emptied broth pot and in it melt the butter. Add the leeks and mushrooms together and gently fry them until lightly coloured. Shake the flour over them and stir around for a few minutes until the flour has been cooked a little. Now, slowly add the reduced hot stock, stirring all the time, until it begins to thicken. Allow to simmer for 15–20 minutes until smooth and the sauce is glossy looking. Check for salt (it should be seasoned enough from the stock cube) and stir in the parsley, plenty of pepper and, finally, the cream. Pour over the chicken meat and carefully mix together. Leave to cool completely.

Remove the pastry from the fridge and, laterally, cut a slice of about one third off the full size, which will be for the lid of the pie. Roll out the remaining two thirds to a thickness of about 3mm. Grease the tart tin and fit in the pastry base, allowing the edge to slightly stand proud from the rim. Generously prick the base of the pastry with a fork, then roll the remaining pastry to the same thickness.

•

Fill the pie with the cooled filling and then brush the edges with the egg/milk mixture. Lay over the lid. Press the pastry well down on the filling (this helps the pie to cook more evenly), then firmly press the overhanging pastry edges together. Take a small, sharp knife and trim off the excess pastry to achieve a neat finish. Brush the surface with more of the egg/milk wash and mark the pastry rim with the tines of a fork; if you wish you may also score the surface of the pastry with the back of a small knife to create a lattice effect. Make two small holes in the centre of the pie to allow steam to escape, then slide the pie on to the baking sheet and cook for 25 minutes.

•

Now, turn the temperature down to 180°C/gas mark 4 and continue cooking for a further 30–40 minutes or so. If the pie is browning too much towards the end of the cooking time, loosely cover with a sheet of foil. Once the pie is a perfect golden brown, allow to rest for about 10 minutes before serving with the delicious carrots and peas (see recipe overleaf).

Stewed carrots and peas

SERVES 4

400g carrots, peeled
50g butter
6 sprigs of mint
a little salt and freshly ground white pepper
1 tsp sugar
400g frozen peas (not petit pois; rather, a larger size)

Thinly slice the carrots (a mandoline is useful, here) at a slight angle and put into a roomy saucepan. Cover with water by about 2cm and add 25g of the butter, two of the mint sprigs, a little salt and pepper and the sugar. Bring up to a simmer, cover and cook slowly for 10 minutes, or until nearly tender. Remove the mint sprigs, add the peas, cover once more and continue to cook – stew, in fact – for a further 10 minutes. Remove the lid and turn up the heat a little. Allow the remaining liquid to reduce until it's nicely coating the vegetables and the peas have lost their bright colour somewhat; I like to take them until they are more the colour of tinned peas, the taste of which I very much enjoy. Now remove the leaves from the remaining four sprigs of mint and finely chop. To finish the dish, stir in the mint, check the seasoning and stir in the remaining 25g of butter. Serve very hot in a deep serving dish alongside the pie, at table.

Marmalade queen of puddings

SERVES 4

NOTE: YOU WILL NEED A DEEP BAKING DISH, APPROX. 1.5 LITRE CAPACITY.

275ml milk
finely grated zest of 1 orange and 1 lemon
100g caster sugar, plus a little extra for sprinkling over the surface of the meringue as it cooks
pinch of salt
50g fresh white breadcrumbs
2 large eggs, separated
a little softened butter, for greasing the dish
4 tbsp best marmalade, preferably not too chunky
very cold pouring cream, to serve

Warm the milk with the orange and lemon zest, remove from the heat, cover and leave to infuse for 30 minutes, until lukewarm. Add 50g of the sugar, the salt, breadcrumbs and egg yolks and mix together thoroughly. Lightly butter the deep baking dish and pour in the mixture. Leave for 15 minutes to allow the crumbs to swell.

•

Preheat the oven to 180°C/gas mark 4.

•

Place the dish in a deep roasting tin and pour in hot tap water to halfway up the sides of the dish to make a bain-marie. Bake in the oven for 25–30 minutes or until set and firm to the touch. Remove from the bain-marie and leave to rest for at least 15 minutes.

Meanwhile, beat the egg whites until stiff, then start to add the remaining 50g of caster sugar in a thin stream. Continue beating until thick and glossy. Spoon the marmalade over the bready sponge, covering the whole surface, and then pile the meringue on top. Shape with the back of a spoon into soft peaks and sprinkle all over with a little more caster sugar. Return the pudding to the oven for about 7–10 minutes, or until pale golden and the surface is lightly crusted. Leave to cool until lukewarm. Serve with very cold pouring cream.

Easter Day

Mimosa

·

Tarte flambée

·

Potted shrimps

·

Asparagus with sauce mousseline

Roast best end of lamb with creamed spinach

·

Hot cross bun bread & butter pudding

Menu introduction

The Mimosa cocktail remains, for me, the preferable name to describe the juice from a freshly squeezed orange carefully mixed with very cold champagne. Buck's Fizz, the naming of which, I believe, was by a bartender at Buck's Club, London, in the 1920s, simply doesn't quite have the same élan, although it pre-dates the Parisian-beau-monde Mimosa offered some years later. My favourite, however – as with almost all expertly made drinks anywhere – is the one made at Harry's Bar in Venice. Here, they further introduce a trickle of Cointreau to their Mimosa, making it special indeed. And, after all, a properly made Mimosa has all that sunshine yellow about it that mimics the flower of the same name. Sadly, the original has since had to endure the attachment of a 1980s Eurovision pop group, so further traducing its rather more elegant past.

'La Tarte Flambée' is a well-known Alsatian speciality, and almost as well known in that region of France as pizza is in the vicinity of Naples, in Italy. Well... maybe not quite. However, that which causes me to be all of a wobble is quite how this most delicious of savoury creations had completely passed me by until I sat down to lunch at The Delaunay, a fine London restaurant, about 18 months ago. Some will say that it is the sister of The Wolseley, in Piccadilly – and I will, too.

Now that I have given myself over to much research since then, it pleases me greatly to see that The Delaunay 'tarte' eschews anything other than the original ingredients. A thin dough not unlike that used for a pizza, but with less yeast, I think (I have never made pizza, mainly because I become tired of eating it just before I get halfway through). Then, a generous smear of crème fraîche upon the thinly rolled wide circle of raw dough, which is then covered with a slew of very softly, butter-stewed, finely chopped white onions and, finally, a scattering of tiny cubes of smoked streaky bacon. And, strictly speaking, I guess, this may be 'ventrèche d'Alsace', the excellent smoked bacon

of the region, but a good one it must be and purchased as a piece and hand-cut; ready-diced pancetta cubes are far too big.

And many thanks must go to Lee Ward, chef at The Delaunay, who generously furnished me with the recipe. Also to the restaurant's proprietors, Chris Corbin and Jeremy King, who, presumably, allowed him to pass it on. I have also slightly adapted their recipe to fit this Easter menu: as a delicious nibble to have with the Mimosa.

I adore little brown shrimps. And, so much so, that they make two appearances in this book. For a perfect Easter first course they are going to be traditionally potted, and as a middle course in the summer lunch menu (see page 135), paired with warm leeks and dill. Now then, please don't *ever* warm potted shrimps before serving them, as some restaurants are wont to do these days, as I feel that this destroys the whole reason for potting them in the first place: the cold and crisp disc of butter, once detached from the shrimps, is perfect for spreading on to hot toast (no extra butter needed, therefore) before piling a few shrimps atop this lactic smear. A quick squirt of lemon juice, a grind of pepper and you're done. Heaven.

Depending on where Easter falls in the calendar, English asparagus should be in the shops. I occasionally pick my own in the Surrey countryside, affording an ultra-fresh taste together with a grand time cutting them from the earth. If the delicious *sauce mousseline* is a new one to you, I feel sure that it will soon become a firm favourite. Essentially, mousseline is a light and airy hollandaise – mousse-like, if you will – and made so by the addition of both loosely beaten cream and, in the initial fabrication of said sauce, a whole egg together with the traditional yolks that are usually used in full. It is less cloying than regular hollandaise (although delicious in itself). Unusually for me, I prefer to take the modern approach and make mousseline sauce in a small food processor; this gives extra air, particularly to the whole egg.

A neat and tidy, well-trimmed best end of lamb is the little darling of the restaurant chef. Perfect portion control, quick to cook and as well behaved as the charming head waiter who quietly coaxes one to choose it from the menu. Usually, it will be offered as a dish to feed two, as a best end normally comes in a rack of eight cutlets, so conveniently giving each diner four of them to tackle – and chewing the bones is, for this guest, *de rigueur*. Creamed spinach is one of the very best of all dishes that utilise these versatile green leaves. And I see no need to offer anything else here.

I don't think I know anyone who doesn't occasionally enjoy a richly comforting bread and butter pudding, and what could be a more fitting occasion to put one on the table than Easter, especially when it's made with hot cross buns. And it's an excellent way of using up those that have been left over, once the little gannets (greedy children, and grown-ups, too) have had their Good Friday fill.

Long gone are the days when bread and butter pudding was made simply from stale bread spread with butter. Now it seems that the more exotic the bread – and usually always fresh, too – the better; panettone and brioche, say. Some even use recipes involving sourdough, which, for me, absolutely doesn't work as it is too tight and chewy; delicious to eat, but not to cook again. I have used a ginger loaf in the past with great success, but my first-ever published recipe used teacakes. That which makes them ideal, of course, is that they already have spice and dried fruit baked within, rather than more traditionally adding currants and sultanas, say, to the assembly in their own right. And, if we are honest, is not the hot cross bun the Pascal teacake?

Mimosa

MAKES 4

NOTE: IT IS EASIER TO MAKE THE MIMOSAS IF YOU USE LARGE FLUTES,
AS IT WILL FACILITATE THE MIXING THEREOF.

4 ice cubes
Cointreau
juice of 4–5 large oranges, strained
1 bottle of well-chilled champagne

Pop a cube of ice into each glass and add a trickle of Cointreau. Then pour in enough orange juice to come about halfway up the flute. Now, slowly top up with champagne and carefully stir. Serve forthwith. (There should be enough juice and champagne left over to offer top-ups.)

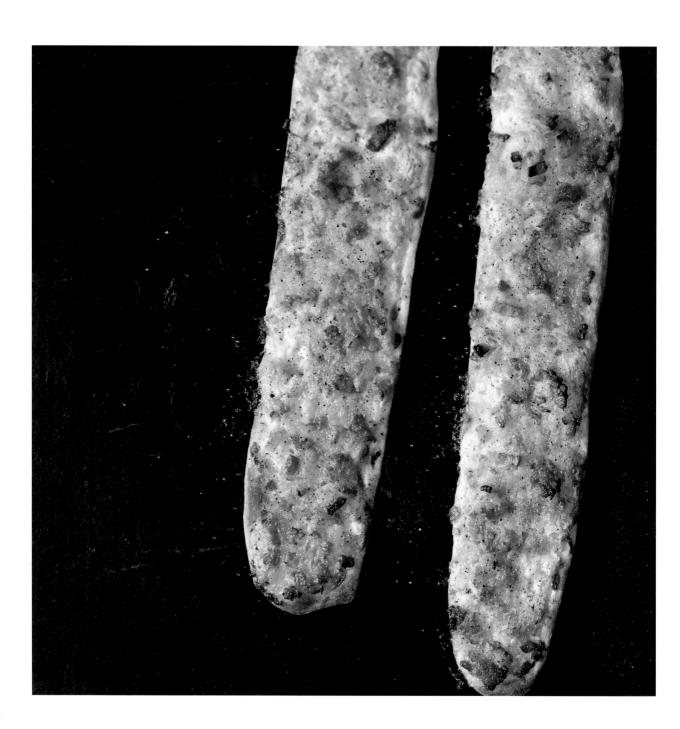

Tarte flambée

SERVES 4

NOTE: YOU WILL NEED A PASTA-ROLLING MACHINE FOR THIS RECIPE. ALSO, IT IS IMPRACTICAL TO MAKE A SMALLER AMOUNT OF DOUGH THAN THAT GIVEN HERE, SO FREEZE THE REMAINDER; THIS IS EXPLAINED LATER IN THE METHOD.

FOR THE DOUGH:

350g strong white bread flour
1 tsp fast-action yeast
1 tsp fine salt
200ml lukewarm water
a little oil, for greasing the dough and tray

FOR THE TOPPING:

30g butter
1 large white onion (or certainly not a red- or pink-fleshed one), finely chopped
100g smoked streaky bacon, finely chopped
100g crème fraîche
freshly ground black pepper

Put the flour, yeast and salt into the bowl of an electric mixer and mingle together with your hand. Pour in the water and start to mix with the dough hook. Allow to mix slowly, then turn up the speed a touch to allow a homogeneous dough to form. If your machine is an efficient one, you should be able to do all the kneading here, for about 5 minutes. (My ancient contraption is inefficient, so I always give the dough a thorough hand-kneading for a few minutes afterwards, but then this is something I particularly enjoy doing anyway.) Tip the dough out of the mixing bowl, then grease it a little so that it doesn't stick while rising. Put back into the mixing bowl, then cover with a damp tea towel and leave somewhere warm for about an hour, so that the dough may rise and double its original size.

Meanwhile, to make the tarte topping gently stew the onions in the butter over a low–medium heat using a solid-based pan, until almost soft and not coloured; about 25–30 minutes. Tip in the bacon and thoroughly stir together with the onions. Continue to cook, with the heat only just a touch more brisk so that the fat runs from the bacon into the onions and mingles nicely together, for a further 5 minutes or so; allow only the slightest golden look to the whole mass, then tip out of the pan into a bowl to cool, scraping out every scrap.

•

Once the dough has risen, tip it out on to a work surface and knock it back to its original size. Using a set of scales (preferably digital), cut the dough into roughly 40–43g pieces, weighing them as you go. If you adhere to this mildly exacting chore, you should end up with 12 pieces. Although you will only need four for this recipe, the remaining eight pieces can be frozen in a plastic box for further renditions.

•

Take a baking tray (without raised edges and completely flat) and very lightly coat it with oil using your hands. Place in the freezer. Now place four pieces of dough on to a plate and put in the fridge to firm up a bit, for 20 minutes. Once they are firm, use a pasta-rolling machine to run each piece of dough through all the rolling grades of diminishing thickness until you reach '5'. At this point the pieces will be thin and resemble a length of pasta, but not quite thin enough. At this '5' stage, pass each length of dough through the rollers three or four times, lay them to rest for a moment and then give each one a final pass; you will notice, now, that they will have all become even thinner and their previous, natural elasticity is very much reduced.

•

Lay these tarte bases on to a floured work surface. Now remove the oiled baking tray from the freezer, immediately lay the bases upon it and return to the freezer. Note: this freezing is important, as the dough needs to be hard for when the cream and topping are spread upon them. If at room temperature, it will be almost impossible to spread them as the dough will ruck up.

•

Preheat the oven to 220°C/gas mark 7.

•

Take the tray from the freezer and, working briskly, spread a thinnish layer of crème fraîche over each base, working the cream almost to the edges. Now take about a tablespoon of the onion/bacon mixture and spread it over the cream, once again almost to the edges. Grind black pepper over each tarte. Slide the tray on to the top shelf of the oven and bake for 5–6 minutes or until the tartes are bubbling, golden, slightly scorched at the edges and smelling absolutely gorgeous. Allow to cool slightly, cut into finger-sized slices and serve with the Mimosas.

Potted shrimps

SERVES 4

NOTE: YOU WILL NEED 4 RAMEKINS.

175g best-quality unsalted butter
350g brown shrimps
a little salt
scant ½ tsp cayenne pepper
¼ tsp ground mace
generous scraping of nutmeg
juice of ½ a lemon

In a large frying pan, melt 100g of the butter. When hot but not frothing, tip in the shrimps and stir around until heated through. Sprinkle with a little salt and stir in the spices. Squeeze in the lemon juice and remove from the heat.

•

Take four ramekins and divide the buttery shrimps between them, making sure you include an equal amount of liquid and butter to the collection of shrimps in each pot. Gently press down with the back of a spoon so that the shrimps are as submerged as possible. Place in the fridge to cool. Once cold, melt the remaining 75g of butter and, dividing it equally between each pot, pour over to seal and then return to the fridge. They will be just fine stored here for up to 3 days.

Asparagus with sauce mousseline

SERVES 4

200g unsalted butter
1 egg
1 egg yolk
juice of 1 small lemon
20 asparagus spears, trimmed and peeled
150ml double cream
salt and freshly ground white pepper

Put the butter in a small saucepan (preferably with a pouring lip) to melt over a low heat. Place the egg, egg yolk, lemon juice and seasoning into the bowl of a small food processor. Switch on and allow the mixture to become very thick and pale in colour; about 3–4 minutes should do it. Meanwhile, reheat the butter until just beginning to bubble a bit, then remove any scum from the surface with a spoon. With the motor still running, slowly add the hot butter (it *must* be hot) to the egg mixture until it visibly begins to thicken. Once the butter has been exhausted and you can see a modicum of milky residue left behind, stop pouring. Tip the sauce into a roomy bowl and keep warm.

Now, boil the asparagus in well salted water for about 5 minutes, or until tender when pierced with a sharp knife; *please* don't undercook them, as I think there is nothing worse than crunchy asparagus! Once cooked, lift them out with a slotted spoon, briefly drain on a tea towel and then place on a warmed serving platter.

·

Finally, briefly hand-whip (preferably) the cream until only loosely thick, so that it is just showing the shape of the spokes in the cream. Carefully fold the cream into the warm sauce using a spatula and then check for both a possible addition of more lemon juice and seasoning. Spoon into a bowl and serve alongside the asparagus, at table.

Roast best end of lamb
with creamed spinach

SERVES 4

2 best ends of lamb (8 ribs preferably, or 6 for a smaller serving),
bones scraped clean, 1–1.2kg trimmed weight
olive oil
salt and freshly ground white pepper

FOR THE CREAMED SPINACH:
800g spinach, well washed and drained
60g butter
2 small shallots, finely chopped
1 tbsp Pernod
1 level tbsp plain flour
150ml whipping cream
a little freshly grated nutmeg

Preheat the oven to 200°C/gas mark 6.

•

Firstly, cook the spinach. Have a large pot of lightly salted boiling water to hand, as well as a large bowl of iced water. Plunge the spinach into the boiling water, bring back to a boil, then immediately drain in a colander. Refresh in the iced water until fully cold, then drain once more and squeeze out all remaining moisture with clutched hands, until quite dry. Now, coarsely chop the spinach and put to one side.

•

Rub a little olive oil over the best ends and season. Place in a roasting tin (fat-side down) and put on to the top shelf of the oven. Roast for 10 minutes, then turn the lamb over (the lamb fat should now be turning crisp and golden) and roast for a further 10–15 minutes. Depending upon the size of the best ends, a smaller one should now be a good rosy pink within; if a little weightier, roast for a further 5 minutes or so. Remove from the oven and allow to rest, loosely covered with foil.

•

To finish the spinach, melt the butter in a roomy saucepan and in it fry the shallots until pale golden. Add the Pernod and allow it to bubble. Stir in the flour and cook for a minute or two, stirring constantly. Pour in the cream, add nutmeg and pepper and stir until simmering. Add the spinach, stir together and reheat for a few minutes until creamy. Finally, check for seasoning and serve nice and hot with the lamb, carved into cutlets.

Hot cross bun
bread and butter pudding

SERVES 4

100g softened, salted butter
4 hot cross buns, cut horizontally and then in half
2 eggs
2 egg yolks
50g caster sugar, plus a little extra to finish
1 tsp vanilla extract
400ml whipping cream
3 tbsp dark rum
whole nutmeg
ice-cold pouring cream, to serve

Using a little of the softened butter, grease a deep-ish baking dish. Spread the remaining butter on to the buns and arrange them in the dish stacked up against each other, cut side uppermost, for preference. Beat the eggs, yolks, sugar and vanilla extract together in a bowl until light and frothy. Pour in the cream and rum and whisk them together until smooth. Pour this over the buttered buns and leave it to soak into them for at least 30 minutes, or even longer, if you like; this will make the pudding that much softer and fondant, once baked. Preheat the oven to 180°C/gas mark 4.

Finally, grate over plenty of nutmeg and sprinkle with the extra caster sugar. Cook in the oven for about 30–35 minutes, or until the pudding is nicely puffed and the surface is gorgeously crusted and golden. Serve just warm, for best results, and not without some ice-cold pouring cream spooned over each serving.

A grand fish lunch

Gibson

·

Fried whitebait

·

Marinated sea bass with lime, chilli
& coriander, with avocado cream

·

A little lobster salad

·

Peppered hake cutlet

·

Buttered parsley pilaf

·

Vanessa's currant tart

Menu introduction

In essence, the Gibson cocktail is a dry martini garnished with tiny, pickled silver skin onions. The first reference to the drink is said to date from around the first decade of the 1900s when, apparently, there were also bitters included in the basic vermouth/gin mix and stirred over ice as usual. The drink was then strained into a glass; three onions were impaled on a cocktail stick and the bartender would slide this into the drink. And, you know, that's about all there is to it. I have never previously added bitters to a Gibson, but I think it sounds rather a good idea – and a nicely old-fashioned one, too.

To the novice, the very idea of a pickled onion in a drink may sound odd, even distasteful. Be assured, however, this piquant little addition soon becomes most appealing and it makes a nice change from the ubiquitous olive, which has never been my bag, to be honest. And, to eat with this perky cocktail, what could be nicer than a plate of cheerfully crisp little fish? The combination of the gin-soaked pickled onion and salty whitebait is a particularly pleasing one.

Something very elegant and subtle is called for after that spirited opener, I feel. I'm not quite sure as to when we, as curious and open-minded gourmet consumers, first began to be intrigued by the idea of a plate of thinly sliced raw fish, most often judiciously dressed with a sharp and oily lotion. I guess the most obvious reason stems from a growing love of all things culinarily Japanese, although it would surely have been the novelty of sushi that started all of that, with its little bolster of rice helping to almost disguise the shock of putting raw tuna, or salmon, say, into one's, how shall we say, uninitiated gob.

My dear friend, the chef Rowley Leigh, astonished me some time ago (possibly 20 of our Earth years, even) with a truly wonderful plate of marinated raw fish: thinly sliced, best-quality tuna dressed up with a deeply savoury amalgam of finely chopped ginger, shallots, garlic, soy sauce and some neutral oil to lightly homogenise this ace assembly. It is, without doubt, one of my most favourite of all Rowley's creations.

Further inspiration in a similar vein – some spanking-fresh raw sea bass in this case – came my way one sunny lunchtime at The River Café in west London, a little more recently. Here, they refer to it as 'carpaccio' of sea bass, often pairing it with seasonal cherry tomatoes and a little dried red chilli. This beautiful plate of fish is then sharpened with a touch of lemon juice and lubricated with some of their finest olive oil. A delight.

Any fish served raw must, clearly, be super-fresh – and cut from a wild fish. Farmed sea bass (from Anglesey last time I saw some), often on offer in almost all supermarkets, is the sorry black sheep, flavour-wise. Very fresh-looking they may be, sometimes, but they have almost no discernable taste – particularly when eaten raw, and little better when cooked. A good fishmonger's is the place to go, and I know full well that finding one is becoming harder and harder. But persevere you should for this dish. The fishmonger will also, hopefully, slice it from a fine wild fillet ready for use.

All that I usually insist on when eating a cold lobster, is a thick bowl of gorgeous mayonnaise served alongside. It is one of *the* great marriages – and a freshly boiled whole crab, of course, is another. However, however... there is a unique little sauce that will forever be a second, close friend to that default emulsion. It is called 'sauce Courchamps' and, along with some other like-minded chefs, cooks and friends, I discovered this charming recipe amongst the pages of Elizabeth David's *An Omelette and a Glass of Wine.* In this book – possibly my favourite of all her books – it is simply served with hot, boiled lobster, and it is obviously very good indeed. (There is a sweet, historical story that accompanies the recipe, which I am not going to go into here, so buy the book!) However, I consider that small pieces of just warm, cooked lobster, a few perfect salad leaves, together with this unusually good sauce, will do justice to the more robust whole hot lobster.

Fresh hake, when I was growing up in Bury, Lancashire, was always, but always there to buy from the fish stalls in the town's wonderful market. As a family, we would probably have it three or four times a month, usually simply cooked in milk and butter or, of course, with parsley sauce (a big bunch of parsley came free with fish, then, as the only sauce anyone really knew, was the parsley one).

But where has all the hake gone now? Well, there was plenty when I visited Bury a couple of years ago, but down south? Almost *nada* – as they say in Spain, where most of our hake is now exported, it being that country's favourite catch of all. Which is all a great shame, for it is a beautiful fish, so pearly white of flesh, once cooked, with its large flakes all so succulent and juicy.

Vanessa Bentley worked on the pastry section at Bibendum over 20 years ago. She came to London from Australia, where she had been working for a friend of mine in his restaurant. So admiring of this tart was he, that it was featured on the menu as 'Vanessa's Currant Tart' – an accolade of which she could be rightly proud. And, if I remember rightly, we also did her proud, too, attaching her name in exactly the same way for the Bibendum dessert menu. It is a sumptuous tart, with an almost 'crème brûlée' type of custard beneath a layer of boozy currants. Tarts don't come much better than this one.

Gibson

MAKES 4

300ml Plymouth gin (my favourite)
plenty of ice, briefly rinsed
50ml dry vermouth
4 shakes Angostura bitters
a jar of silver skin onions (the Opies brand is very good)
cocktail sticks

First of all, have the gin in the fridge and glasses ready-chilled in the freezer. Now fill a large cocktail shaker (or glass jug) with plenty of ice. Add the vermouth and bitters, then pour over the gin. Mix well for about a minute, so that it is very cold. Strain into the chilled glasses, impale three onions on to a cocktail stick and slide into the drink. Serve without delay.

Fried whitebait

SERVES 4

NOTE: IT IS ESSENTIAL TO OWN A HOUSEHOLD DEEP-FRYER FOR THIS RECIPE.

oil, for deep-frying
500g whitebait (a good frozen brand is just fine, simply defrost them before use)
milk
4–5 tbsp plain flour
½ tsp cayenne pepper
1 tsp fine sea salt
lemons, to serve

Preheat the oil in the deep-fryer to 180–190°C.

•

Put the whitebait into a bowl and pour enough milk over them to just cover. Leave them submerged for 10 minutes or so, then drain in a colander or sieve. Discard the milk. Tip the flour into a large plastic bag, add the cayenne pepper and salt and shake together. Now add the drained whitebait, toss them around in the bag while shaking well until each and every tiny fish is thoroughly coated.

Now then, suspend the frying basket over the sink and then lift small handfuls of flour-coated fish directly into the basket – but only fry half the fish at a time; over-crowding the fryer when cooking whitebait can result in a sorry mess of soggy fish, mainly due to a lowering of temperature. Carefully lower the basket into the oil and fry for no more than 1–2 minutes, or until the fish are pale golden and super-crisp: they should rustle well, when shaken. Drain on to folded kitchen paper, then fry the remaining fish. Serve with halves of lemon.

Marinated sea bass
with lime, chilli and coriander,
with avocado cream

SERVES 4

350–400g fillet of wild sea bass, skinned, bones removed
1 heaped tsp sea salt
2 large green chillies (jalapeños if you can find some), deseeded, or not, if you wish, finely chopped
juice of 2 limes
2 tbsp extra virgin olive oil (the very best you can afford)
a dozen or so small sprigs of fresh coriander

FOR THE AVOCADO CREAM:
2 small Hass avocados
5–6 tbsp milk
3 tsp green Tabasco sauce
2 tsp Worcestershire sauce
juice of 1 lime
a little sea salt, to taste

Using a supple, sharp knife slice the fish at an angle quite thinly – as an 'escalope', if you like. Lay on to a serving platter that is large enough to accommodate all the fish in a single layer. Evenly sprinkle over the salt and chillies, then squeeze over the lime juice. Leave to macerate in the fridge while you make the avocado cream. Place all the ingredients in a small food processor and purée until very smooth. Turn out into a pretty bowl, cover with clingfilm and chill in the fridge for 30 minutes.

•

To finish the dish, spoon the olive oil over the sea bass, then carefully remove the leaves from the sprigs of coriander and prettily place all over the macerated fish. Serve at table, with the avocado cream handed separately.

A little lobster salad

SERVES 4

*1 x 850g–1kg cooked hen lobster (it is essential that it is a female lobster,
as the roe within is used in the dressing for the salad)
2 simple round lettuces, outer leaves removed and discarded,
revealing only the central, paler green leaves*

FOR THE DRESSING:
*1 small shallot, finely chopped
the leaves from 2 sprigs of tarragon, finely chopped
the leaves from 3 sprigs of parsley, finely chopped
1 tsp smooth Dijon mustard
2 tsp anisette de Bordeaux (available from some good wine shops
or online; a bottle of it keeps for months)
juice of ½ small lemon
2 tsp light soy sauce
4–5 tbsp extra virgin olive oil
freshly ground black pepper*

Take the lobster and split it down its length with a sharp and heavy knife (if you are unsure about doing this, then ask the fishmonger to do it at the time of purchase). Remove the gritty stomach sack in the head and then scoop the creamy parts out into a bowl. Remove the more firm and bright red roe, chop it very finely and also add it to the bowl. Put to one side. Now remove all the meat from the tail of the lobster and crack the claws with a rolling pin, say. Remove the meat from these, too, and, if possible, keep them in one piece. Also put these to one side. Wash the lettuce leaves, dry them well and arrange on four pretty plates.

To make the dressing, add the shallot, tarragon and parsley to the bowl containing the lobster roe and creamy parts. Add black pepper, the mustard, anisette, lemon juice and soy sauce, then whisk all together until well amalgamated and smooth-ish. Now begin to whisk in the olive oil as a thin stream until a loose dressing has been achieved; the taste should be very slightly sweet and sharp.

To serve, slice the lobster meat into small pieces and divide it equally among the lettuce leaves. Spoon over the dressing, but do not drown the salad.

Peppered hake cutlet

SERVES 4

1 tbsp white peppercorns
1 tbsp black peppercorns
4 hake cutlets, approx. 200g each
a little plain flour
2 tbsp olive oil
25g butter
2 tbsp cognac
4 tbsp strong, well-flavoured chicken stock
1 tbsp double cream
a squeeze of lemon juice
salt

Using a coffee grinder, or similar, coarsely grind the peppercorns, then put into a sieve and shake off excess fine powder which, if included, will make the dish far too 'hot'. Now sprinkle the sieved pepper over one surface of the hake cutlets, press in well with the fingers and put to one side, on a plate.

Lightly dust the peppered side of the hake cutlets with flour and season with salt. Put the oil and the butter in a large frying pan and, when just beginning to froth, slide in the cutlets, peppered-side down. Cook for about 3–4 minutes and then carefully turn over. Continue cooking for a few minutes more, or until the central bone of the fish may be eased away from the flesh when nudged with a fork. Peel off the skin that surrounds each cutlet, then remove the hake to a warmed serving dish, cover with foil and keep warm.

Pour the cognac into the frying pan, allow it to bubble for a few minutes, then add the stock. Over a medium heat, stir together and reduce until syrupy. Now pour in the cream and stir once more to make a smooth sauce. Add a small squeeze of lemon juice to finish. Take the foil off the fish, where you will find a modicum of fishy juices. Tip these into the sauce, also stir in and then pour over the cutlets. Serve at once, together with the buttered parsley pilaf (recipe overleaf).

Buttered parsley pilaf

SERVES 4

plenty of ice cubes
1 bunch of curly parsley (the larger ones found in the supermarkets), coarser stems discarded
80g butter
1 small clove of garlic, crushed
4 spring onions, trimmed and finely chopped
200g basmati rice (I use the Tilda brand, and never wash it)
320ml water
salt and freshly ground white pepper

Preheat the oven to 180°C/gas mark 4.

•

Fill a large bowl with cold water and then add to it about a dozen ice cubes.

•

Bring a large pot of salted water to a rolling boil and plunge in the parsley sprigs. Almost bring back to a boil, then strain through a sieve over the sink. Quickly rinse under a cold running tap then plunge the blanched parsley into the iced water and stir it around a bit. Leave there for a couple of minutes, strain once more and squeeze the parsley with your hand until no water remains.

•

Now, melt 50g of the butter then allow to cool for a minute or two. Pour into a small food processor, add the parsley and crushed garlic to it and process together until very smooth and a vivid green. Put to one side, still in the processor bowl.

Melt the remaining butter in a roomy pot that also has a tight-fitting lid. Add the spring onions and cook gently without colouring them. Tip in the rice and stir around in the butter and spring onions until well coated. Pour in the water and slowly bring up to a simmer. Add a little salt and pepper and, once the rice is simmering, put on the lid and slide into the oven. Cook for 15 minutes.

•

Remove from the oven, **don't lift off the lid**, and leave to sit for 5 minutes. Now take off the lid and stir in the buttery parsley purée until the entire pot of rice is a gorgeous green. Now lay a tea towel over the pan and then clamp the lid on tight. Rest for another 5 minutes, allowing the rice to steam, which will be absorbed by the towel. Finally, remove the lid and towel, stir together once more and serve with the hake.

Vanessa's currant tart

SERVES 4

NOTE: YOU WILL NEED A 20 X 4CM TART TIN.

125g currants
100g Armagnac

FOR THE PASTRY:
125g plain flour
75g cold unsalted butter, diced
2 rounded tbsp icing sugar
pinch of salt
1 egg yolk mixed with a trickle of iced water
2 eggs, beaten, to glaze

FOR THE CUSTARD FILLING:
300ml whipping cream
½ tsp vanilla extract
2 egg yolks
2 eggs
25g caster sugar
pinch of salt
freshly grated nutmeg

First soak the currants in the Armagnac. It is best to weigh the currants in a dish and then simply pour in the given weight of spirit. Leave to soak for at least 2 hours, or overnight, or for simply ages in a preserving jar. In fact, why not soak a lot of currants in Armagnac, so that they are always to hand for making this delicious tart whenever you feel the urge; the alcohol-soaked dried fruit will keep almost indefinitely.

In a food processor, electric mixer or manually, blend together the flour, butter, icing sugar and salt until it resembles fine breadcrumbs. Now tip into a large, roomy bowl and gently mix in the egg yolk/water mix until all is well amalgamated. Put into a plastic bag and chill in the fridge for at least 1 hour before rolling.

Preheat the oven to 180°C/gas mark 4, together with a flat baking sheet, as this will help cook the base of the pastry.

Roll out the pastry as thinly as possible, line a 20 x 4cm deep tart tin and blind bake. To do this, line the uncooked pastry case with a sheet of foil and fill with some dried beans, for instance. Bake on the heated baking sheet for about 15–20 minutes, remove from the oven and transfer the foil and beans to a bowl or tin (for future use). Brush the inside of the case with the beaten egg, which will form a seal and prevent any leaks. Return to the oven for a further 10 minutes or so, until it is pale golden, crisp and well cooked through, particularly the base. Remove from the oven and turn down the temperature to 170°C/gas mark 3.

•

Now, warm together the cream and vanilla extract in a saucepan. Beat together the egg yolks, eggs and sugar and then add the vanilla-flavoured cream. Add the salt, lightly whisk together and leave to stand for 5 minutes. Lift off any froth with some kitchen paper and then carefully ladle almost all the mixture into the cooked pastry case. Place again on the heated baking sheet on the middle shelf of the oven, slightly pulled out, and then add the rest of the custard (this is simply a good way of avoiding spillage). Bake for 30 minutes. Remove – it should still be a bit wobbly – and dust the surface with plenty of freshly grated nutmeg. Return to the oven and finish cooking for a further 10 minutes until well set. Cool completely before generously covering the surface with the soaked currants. Once the currants have been added, eat within an hour or so. Note: if the currants seem particularly wet, drain briefly in a sieve before using.

A cosy supper after the show

French 75

·

Spiced almonds

·

A cup of beef tea with Madeira

·

Bacon du Bedat

·

Jansson's temptation

·

Vanilla custard pots

Menu introduction

It was the English bartender of the Hemingway Bar at the Paris Ritz, one Colin Field, who made me my first French 75. It was early evening, about 6.30, and I was on my way out to meet friends for an early dinner at Chez Georges, a favourite, truly traditional Parisian restaurant (some call it a bistro, but it is classier than that) a 15-minute stroll away. Anyway, I needed a sharpener.

'Don't know what to have', I said to Colin. 'Well, I think I know just the thing.' Out of the freezer came a tall flute and in went some gin, a touch of sugar syrup, lemon juice, topped up with champagne. It was just the ticket. 'Knew you would like it', said Colin, as I handed over more euros than was perhaps sensible... But it *was* absolutely delicious! Note: it is important that all components of the drink are as chilled as possible, including the all-important glass itself.

Something so refreshing, a touch sweet and with a hidden hit from the gin, calls for some salt and crunch; a kind of surreptitious, occasional graze from a wandering hand, let us say. Good nuts, therefore, are what is needed, here. It is both fun and mildly thrifty to buy one's own nuts – skinned almonds, in this case – and to add a touch of spice to enliven their oily crunch. The spices in the recipe here, are my own personal mix. Feel free, however, to add or remove those that don't appeal, although an overload could result in a whiff of 'Bombay mix', which may ruin the sophistication of the French 75.

I get my nuts from Whole Foods Market in London, where they sell them loose from huge canisters. These nuts pour out at some speed, once a lever has been employed, and cascade into a neat, brown paper bag until the flow is staunched. To me, these appear to be fresh nuts indeed and, to keep them in this state, I store them in the freezer and use whenever the need arises.

I will always remember a friend telling me, years ago, of a post-Glyndebourne performance of Mozart's *Idomeneo*, when he had been invited back to his host's very grand house, just a few miles away from the opera house. Once everyone had assembled in the sitting room, a butler arrived with a tray of beautiful porcelain beakers, filled to the brim with hot – but not steaming – deeply savoury beef tea. It had been an unseasonably cool and rainy evening so, sensibly and, more importantly, thoughtfully, the initial intention of the 'tea' being served cold and, therefore, delightfully jellied, was abandoned. Stylish and considerate hosts, to be sure.

I first read of 'Bacon du Bedat' in an endearing and charming book called *A Pike in the Basement – Tales of a Hungry Traveller*, written by the wine writer (and erstwhile wine trader) Simon Loftus. First published in 1987, it remains one of my favourite food-related books. It is all at once delightful, idiosyncratic and bohemian; in essence, the travel journal of a young man, neatly punctuated by occasional recipes. But it is this curious bacon one that is, for me, the star. So, please don't be shocked by the idea of a toasted sandwich containing bacon, smoked salmon and mango chutney, as it is surprisingly delicious and moreish.

Oh, what a controversial dish is the Jansson's Temptation: a recipe involving thickly cut matchstick potatoes (think thin, short chips) baked with cream, onions and Swedish anchovies and finished with fresh white breadcrumbs, giving a soft crust to the finished dish. Essentially, this is a gentle gratin. I am forever silently shouting at magazine pages, occasional cookery TV programmes and a few restaurant menus, too – although with regard to the latter, it is only when the promised dish arrives at table, bearing no relation whatsoever to that of the dish promised, that I become vocal in reality.

A true Jansson's only, but *only* uses the Swedish 'anchovy' (it is a sprat, in fact). These are as different to the southern European anchovy as caviar is to lumpfish roe; this has nothing at all to do with an obvious cost ratio, here, simply taste and texture. But, for Heaven's sake and once and for all, the familiar (to us), delicious oily salted anchovy has no place at all in this fabulous Swedish creation! I have lost count of the times I have read '... and if you can't find Swedish anchovies, then the usual ones will be just as good'. *Just As Good?* They. Are. Not. The. Same. And not ever.

Yes, the Swedish anchovy/sprat fillets are sold in tins (the only similarity), but these are immersed in a brine (as opposed to oil), which is also a touch sweet, which is typically Scandinavian with almost all preserved fish. They are also very, very soft and even a touch slimy to the touch. But, let me further become angry (ha!) with those who think it is a good idea to include wildly inappropriate garlic, or to ignore the essential chopped onion, or slice whole potatoes thinly as for a 'gratin Dauphinois', or completely forget to strew the dish, prior to sliding it into the oven, with those all-important fresh white breadcrumbs, which gives the finished 'temptation' such a lovely, gentle crust into which a large serving spoon is just waiting to delve. Will that do?

To finish this late *soirée*, I can only envisage something small – dainty, even – and sweet enough to let one know that only an intense, tiny cup of coffee could possibly follow. Vanilla is called for, here, as are eggs, sugar and cream, all nicely set as a tiny, silky-smooth custard pot, to be delicately scooped up with a silver teaspoon. Appropriately, this closing moment should also match the opening, diminutive serving of savoury goodness: in other words, just right.

Perhaps a cognac or two with the coffee... Maybe a cigar... Even a rubber of bridge. But, soon enough, a timely cry will announce that it is, 'Up the stairs to Bedfordshire!'

French 75

MAKES 4

4 ice cubes
120ml gin (Plymouth is my favourite)
4 level tsp caster sugar
8 tsp lemon juice
400–450ml well-chilled champagne
4 maraschino cherries, or 4 strips lemon zest (both optional, but I prefer the lemon zest)

Have four large champagne flutes chilled, then pop an ice cube into each one. Pour over 30ml gin per flute, add a teaspoon of sugar and two teaspoons of lemon juice, and top up with champagne. Add a cherry or a strip of lemon zest, if liked, then carefully stir together.

Spiced almonds

3 tsp caster sugar
1 tsp celery salt
1 tsp sea salt
1 level tsp cayenne pepper
1 level tsp ground cumin
the leaves from a sprig of rosemary
1 small clove of garlic, chopped
300g whole, skinned almonds
3 tsp olive oil

Preheat the oven to 170°C/gas mark 3.

•

In a coffee grinder or similar, process together the first seven ingredients until finely ground. Put the almonds in a roomy bowl, spoon over the olive oil and thoroughly mix together with a rubber spatula until the almonds are glossy. Sprinkle over the spice powder bit by bit, while continuing to mix with the spatula. Once all the almonds are well coated, turn out on to a large, shallow oven tray that will accommodate them in a single layer – or as near to that as possible.

•

Bake in the oven for 10–15 minutes, then remove and turn the almonds over and around with the spatula. Bake for a further 10 minutes or so, until golden and smelling quite gorgeous. Leave to cool in the tray and then serve in pretty bowls. Any leftover nuts should be stored in a sealed plastic box or tin for another day... as if!

A cup of beef tea with Madeira

SERVES 4

1kg beef shin, sawn across the bone by the butcher
into two thick slices
2.5 litres water
250g carrots, peeled and cut into chunks
500g onions, thickly sliced
1 beef stock cube
(I find that the jellied ones are better than an actual cube)
2 bay leaves
200g Madeira, plus a little extra, when serving the beef tea
2 cloves
6 large, dark-gilled mushrooms, cut into quarters
1 tsp sea salt
1 tsp black peppercorns

Preheat the oven to 140ºC/gas mark 1.

Cut away any excess fat from the beef shin, then put it into a large, lidded pot (a Le Creuset is ideal, here) and cover with water (*not* the listed, measured amount). Bring up to a simmer, then remove the beef with tongs and briefly rinse it under running water from the tap. Throw away the water from the pot, rinse it clean and then return the beef to it; this initial process will remove the worst of any impurities (visible as surface scum), which emerge from the beef while it further cooks.

Now, add the measured water and all the remaining ingredients and slowly bring up to a quiet simmer. More unsightly scum will, inevitably, come to the surface – from the vegetables and, would you believe, also from the water itself! So, skim this off with a ladle until the surrounding broth emits less

and less. Once happy, cover the pot and slide it into the oven. Cook for 3 hours, occasionally having a peek to see that the liquid is not cooking too fast, as it should be just ticking over; the quieter the process, the clearer the broth will emerge as the beef and vegetables give off their flavours, so turn the heat down a touch if this is the case.

Once the time is up, remove the pot from the oven. Take off the lid and carefully remove the beef with a slotted spoon (it will be almost falling apart) and put it in on a plate; there will be little flavour left in it so discard it – or perhaps you have a hungry hound? Now, strain the broth and vegetables through a colander into another bowl and allow it to drip for 10 minutes, or so.

Line a sieve with some muslin or a clean tea towel and pour the broth through this into a clean pan, where it will emerge nice and clear. Leave to cool for an hour or so, then remove any fat from the surface (there should be very little) with a few sheets of absorbent kitchen paper. Finally, check for seasoning, and your delicious, savoury 'beef tea' is ready. When you wish to serve it, gently re-heat without boiling, adding a little extra Madeira to each serving.

Bacon du Bedat

SERVES 4

12 thin slices of smoked streaky bacon or good-quality pancetta
8 thin slices of white or brown bread
(I actually quite like it made with sliced Hovis)
soft, unsalted butter
2 scant tbsp mango chutney (I now use the Sharwood's brand squeezy tube)
4 thin slices of smoked salmon
plenty of freshly ground black pepper

Place the bacon on the rack of a grill-pan and quietly cook under a moderate heat, turning once, until crisp and golden. Transfer to a large plate in one layer and keep warm; under the turned-off grill would be a good idea.

·

Now, toast the bread and spread with butter, then generously spread each slice with the mango chutney. Place three slices of the warm bacon on each of four slices, then further top each with a slice of smoked salmon. Finally, top with the remaining four slices of toast and press together well, but gently. Cut off the crusts if you wish (I wish), cut them into fingers and eat forthwith. A rare delight.

Jansson's temptation

SERVES 4

50g softened butter
2 onions, peeled and finely chopped
2 x 125g tins Swedish anchovies, including the juice from only one of the tins
6 medium-sized, red-skinned potatoes (Desiree), peeled, cut into thick matchsticks,
briefly rinsed, well drained and dried
400ml whipping cream
2 tbsp fresh white breadcrumbs
a little salt and some freshly ground white pepper

Preheat the oven to 190°C/gas mark 5.

•

Grease a shallow, ovenproof dish (handsome enough to transfer from oven to table) with half the softened butter. Fill the base of it with the onions. Using a pair of scissors, snip the anchovies into small pieces and distribute them over the onions. Pour over the juice from one of the tins. Cover with the prepared potatoes, press them down lightly and season. Pour over the cream and then quietly tap the dish a couple of times on a wooden surface to settle the assembly. Sprinkle the breadcrumbs evenly over the surface and dot with the remaining softened butter. Bake in the oven for anything between 45 minutes and 1 hour, or until the surface of the dish is nicely gilded, crusted and bubbling around the edges. Serve as is, all on its own.

Vanilla custard pots

SERVES 4

NOTE: YOU WILL NEED 4 RAMEKINS.

300ml single cream
tiny pinch of salt
½ vanilla pod, split in half lengthways
3 egg yolks
50g caster sugar
a little grated nutmeg

Preheat the oven to 170°C/gas mark 3.

Pour the cream into a small pan, then add the salt and vanilla pod. Warm together, occasionally stirring, until just below simmering point. Switch off the heat, cover with a lid and leave to infuse for at least 30 minutes. Put the egg yolks and caster sugar into a roomy bowl, and whisk together until pale in colour. Strain the vanilla-infused cream over the egg mixture (remove the pod, pop it in a lidded jar and cover with caster sugar for another time) while further whisking together until well blended. Return the mixture to the pan and, over a low heat, cook while stirring constantly with a wooden spoon for about 5 minutes, or until you can see that the vanilla seeds are in suspension and the mixture has very slightly thickened. Carefully pour into four small ramekins and then place in a deep roasting tin and fill with hot tap water, so that it rises up the outside of the ramekins by about three quarters.

Grate a little nutmeg over each pot and bake in the oven for about 25 minutes, or until the custards have achieved a wobbly set, are slightly puffed and the scent of the nutmeg coating has become faintly toasted. Remove from the oven, take the custards out of the tin and leave to cool for 20 minutes. Put in the fridge for at least 2 hours, to chill fully. Eat with a teaspoon – and on the day of making, please.

A substantial
late weekend breakfast

Bullshot

·

Devils on horseback

·

Baked mushrooms with tomatoes

·

Kedgeree

·

Veal kidneys on big fried bread

·

Orange & pink grapefruit salad
with Angostura bitters

Menu introduction

I had my first Bullshot at the Bemelmans Bar at The Carlyle Hotel in New York City, mixed by Tommy, the genial Irish bartender. I am told by those who know these things that Tommy is still tending that wonderful bar, even though he must be in his early seventies by now. It was lunchtime, dead on the stroke of midday, and I was suffering from the most ferocious hangover (it had been a very late night at the brasserie, Balthazar), of which I informed Tommy.

'Have you ever had a Bullshot, sir?', he politely enquired. I had heard of the drink, knowing that it was, in essence, a Bloody Mary with the tomato juice removed and replaced with beef consommé. 'Okay, Tommy', I said, 'let's give it a go!'. So off scuttled Tommy to fix me one. Into a cocktail shaker went the vodka over ice; the other usual ingredients followed: Worcestershire sauce, Tabasco, pepper and lime – but no salt, as the consommé would be seasoned enough, said the expert. Lots of shaking followed and then it was poured directly into a fat little glass beaker (the glasses they use at Bemelmans are beautiful and *very* old-style New York), ice and all.

'That looks like a small glass of Guinness', I said. Well, it was just delicious. The vigorous shaking had given the drink a frothy head, with the dark brew lurking beneath. It was so instantly invigorating, savoury, ice-cold and with just the correct amount of 'heat' from the sauces. 'That has truly hit the spot, Tommy. Thank you so much!'. He then told me the secret of a good one: 'Don't put in too much vodka.' Not, I guess, quite the answer I was expecting. Once finished, in seemingly no time at all, however, I ordered another...

The other very important thing Tommy told me was with regard to the consommé. He showed me a small can of Campbell's 'beef broth' that he had used. 'It's the only one', he said, 'because the condensed consommé gels when it's mixed with the ice, whereas the broth is totally liquid.' So, since then, whenever I go to the US I will always bring half a dozen tins of broth home with me – they can be found in almost every corner grocery store to giant marts across the country. Failing that, Baxter's beef consommé in the UK is an alternative, but even that is a touch gelled. I have made my own 'broth', too. And, as luck would have it, the 'beef tea' recipe (see page 214) is exactly that. Make plenty and freeze any left over for making your very own invigorating, brilliant bullshots.

A good and healthy way to begin a late breakfast is, of course, with prunes. Here, however, they are tightly wrapped up in thin slices of streaky bacon, then grilled to a crisp: 'devils on horseback' is their name and very delicious they are too. A very nice sweet/savoury nibble to accompany one's brave bullshot.

Advisedly, I would begin to cook the next course of simply baked mushrooms and tomatoes before you even begin to make the bullshots and grill the 'devils'. Slow roasting them is the order of the day, so that as the mushrooms stew and give off their juices, so too do the tomatoes give up theirs into the fungal cups beneath, while also becoming nicely scorched and intensely flavoured above. The first whiff of a fine breakfast, to be sure.

Kedgeree, ah... lovely kedgeree. A grand late breakfast would, for me, not be complete without this smoky-fish-scented dish of great distinction. This particular kedgeree needs to be light and diminutive, considering that which has gone before and that yet to come. With this in mind, the kedgeree is going to be a dry one, rather than rich and creamy; the latter most usually mixed with a béchamel-style sauce fashioned from the milk used to poach the smoked haddock. And smoked haddock it will most definitely be, as, for me, this is the only smoked fish to use. Smoked salmon may sound luxurious, yes, but when cooked does it not simply taste like any smoked fish? Well, I think it does. Haddock it is, then.

A breakfast feast further deserves a special moment for the main dish; if there is such a thing at breakfast, however late the hour. Though costly and not necessarily easy to come by, kidneys from a calf are possibly the most luxurious of all animal innards: sweet and tender, with a pale pink interior when cooked just so – in other words, not for long.

After cooking, allow them to rest on the fried bread itself, so that the kidney juices will deliciously soak into it. A smear of English mustard is, for this cook, obligatory here.

To finish, it is surely time for some freshness. I am very fond of preparing grapefruits and oranges in neat segments, for breakfast. However much this fiddle may be seen as laborious and exacting to some, it bothers me not one jot; well, I have been doing this kind of thing most of my working life, and so enjoy the precision of such a task.

Not all culinary chores are easy to do, but when a little time and patience is expended upon something so worthwhile – especially when you eventually come to eat it – you will, in retrospect, suddenly realise quite how much fun it all was. Yes? Well, I hope so. A small sharp knife is all that is required, together with a little skill in wielding it within skin, pith and the flesh of the fruit. One last thing: please don't forget to add the Angostura bitters, as they give the salad a particular character all its own.

Bullshot

SERVES 2

ice cubes
50ml vodka
25ml dry sherry
3–4 shakes of Worcestershire sauce, or to taste
3–4 shakes of Tabasco sauce, or to taste
juice of ½ lime
a sprinkle or two of celery salt
150ml beef consommé (Baxter's or homemade 'Beef Tea', see page 214)

Put plenty of ice into a large cocktail shaker and add all the other ingredients. Shake vigorously and strain into small tumblers; the result should resemble small glasses of Guinness. Serve forthwith.

Devils on horseback

MAKES 12

12 pitted prunes, soaked in a bowl of hot, strained tea for 30 minutes
12 very thin slices of pancetta

Drain the prunes well, wrap each one in a slice of pancetta and then place on a baking tray, making sure that you keep the join underneath. Put them under a hot grill and cook for a couple of minutes until the pancetta is just beginning to colour and turn crisp. Turn them over and repeat on the other side. Finally, turn the little devils over once more and grill to a final, sizzling crisp. Serve at once, speared with cocktail sticks for ease of eating.

Baked mushrooms with tomatoes

SERVES 2

1 large ripe beef tomato
2 large dark-gilled open-cap mushrooms
unsalted butter
2 tsp olive oil
salt and freshly ground black pepper

Preheat the oven to 190°C/gas mark 5.

Using a sharp, serrated knife cut two thick horizontal slices from the centre of the tomato. Place the mushrooms cup-side up in a shallow baking dish, add a scrap of butter to the centre of each and lightly season. Cover each mushroom with a slice of tomato, lightly season these, too, then spoon over the olive oil and smear it over the surfaces using your finger. Slide into the oven and bake for about 30–40 minutes, or until the tomatoes have nicely blistered and the base of the dish is all a-mingle with juices from both. Serve at once, on pretty breakfast plates.

Kedgeree

SERVES 2

40g butter
2 small shallots, finely chopped
2 heaped tsp curry powder
130g basmati rice (I always use Tilda and don't wash it)
200ml water
200g undyed smoked haddock fillet, boned and skinned
2 freshly cooked hard-boiled eggs, shelled and sliced while still warm
a little salt and pepper

Preheat the oven to 180°C/gas mark 4.

Melt the butter in a lidded cooking pot. Add the shallots and allow to fry gently for a moment or two over a moderate heat, until just beginning to colour. Stir in the curry powder and sizzle for a minute or so, stirring constantly so that it does not burn. Now tip in the rice and stir around until the grains are well coated with the curry-flavoured butter. Pour in the water and a touch of seasoning. Bring up to a simmer, then slip in the haddock fillet, gently submerging it under the surface. Put on the lid, slide into the oven and bake for

15 minutes. Remove from the oven, then leave to stand for 3 minutes without removing the lid; this is important because it allows the rice and fish to finish cooking.

Take off the lid, and immediately fork the rice about, which will both fluff it and also break up the fish into flakes. Now cover the pot with a tea towel, clamp on the lid, and leave for a further 3 minutes, so allowing excess steam to be absorbed by the towel. Transfer from the pot into a heated serving dish and lay over the sliced eggs. Serve without delay.

Veal kidneys on big fried bread

SERVES 2

1 small veal kidney, trimmed of all central gristle and cut into approx. 2cm slices
3–4 tbsp olive oil
2 large and quite thick slices of country bread (sourdough, pain de campagne or similar)
a little room-temperature butter
smooth Dijon mustard
a little chopped parsley
salt and freshly ground black pepper

Season the kidney slices and brush with a little olive oil on each side. Place in a solid frying pan and cook over a high heat until nicely burnished, and for about a minute on each side; this will produce rare-cooked kidneys, but they will also take some further cooking at the end of the recipe. Place the kidneys on a plate and put to one side.

•

Preheat an overhead grill to medium–hot.

•

Generously brush one side of each bread slice with olive oil and lightly season. Wipe out the same frying pan with a damp cloth and place over a medium heat. Place the bread oil-side down in the pan and begin to fry/toast it. When it is golden-brown remove the bread to a small oven tray, fried/toasted-side down.

•

Now spread the soft, upper side of the bread with butter and then smear generously with the mustard. Evenly place the slices of kidney over the mustard and then rub a little butter over them with your finger. Slide on to a low shelf of the grill and cook for 2–3 minutes, or until the edges of the bread have toasted somewhat, the surface of the kidneys is sizzling and their juices are deliciously seeping into the bread. Serve at once, sprinkled with a little parsley just to pretty the dish.

Orange and pink grapefruit salad with Angostura bitters

SERVES 2

2 large oranges
2 pink grapefruit (or red, if pink are unavailable)
Angostura bitters

Take a sharp serrated knife and cut the top and bottom from both the oranges and the grapefruit to only just reveal the flesh. Standing each fruit on an end, carefully slice off the skin, pith and all, revolving the fruit as you proceed, until all that is left is a naked fruit without any remnants of pith. Now, holding each fruit in one hand and over a bowl, carefully slice between the membranes so that each segment of fruit is released, while also making sure that any pips are removed. Once this pleasing task is complete, squeeze the exhausted frame of the fruit in your hand so that all remaining juices are added to the fruit below. Mix together with the Angostura bitters and place in the fridge, covered, for at least an hour, until well chilled. Decant into a pretty dish and serve with much pride. Deliciously refreshing!

Five favourites

Margarita

·

Guacamole with tortilla chips

·

Cucumber salad

·

Kipper pâté

·

Braised lamb shanks with white beans

·

Pavlova

Menu introduction

There are certain dishes in my cookery life that, for one reason or another, I return to over and over again. It is not just the joy of eating these favourites, but the cooking of them, too; the method, or style even, of their preparation. I see them as old friends, regularly turned out to give pleasure to both myself and others. In the case of the menu here, we have a simple salad, a pâté, a comforting braise and a rich and sweet meringue confection. In an almost ironic way, this may well be the most balanced of all the menus in this book, simply because the courses seem easier on the mind – well, to this cook's mind, anyway.

As with all the menus, we begin with a carefully made cocktail and a nibble (apart from the celebratory supper, where an unusual drink ends the meal; see page 118). In this particular instance we veer away from Continental drinks and travel across the Atlantic for the margarita. It is an astonishingly good drink and has always confounded me in a way, as its base spirit, tequila, is not a tipple that rides high on my list of favourites. In fact, hidden away in a margarita is the only place where I feel at home with tequila – actually, *very* much at home if the truth be told.

During my early years as chef at Bibendum, and while working with a dead keen brigade, they and I would occasionally gather together for a jolly outing. One of our favourites, in those days, was to head for the recently opened Mexican Café Pacifico, in Covent Garden. To use an old-fashioned phrase, it was fun, fun, fun and everyone could let their hair down, including chef...

The waiters were slim-hipped, dead handsome and endearingly cheeky. The constant music was of the 'salsa' school, of which we had never heard but knew that we had listened to it somewhere, sometime; we naturally nudged about to it even while sitting down. And one sat down at long wooden tables, which, although they looked rough and ready, were exactly what the enterprising owners had intended. None of us had ever seen anything like it before. We drank huge, well-iced pitchers of margaritas while also tucking into proper, authentically made guacamole and tortilla chips. Heigh ho!

Many years earlier, and on one of my very first eating trips to Paris, I chose to have lunch at the legendary Left Bank bistro Chez Allard. Opened in 1935, or thereabouts, the kitchen was the domain of Madame Allard, while her husband ran the restaurant. I now imagine that they would have been close to retiring by the time I showed up, but the menu remained a delight. I recall such dishes as her famous *caneton aux olives, coquilles Saint Jacques beurre blanc, saucisson chaud et salade de pommes de terre, cuisses de grenouilles* and, as it was summertime when I was there, a wonderfully simple *salade de concombres*. I urge you to try this unique taste of high summer, when cucumbers are at their most fragrant.

A well-made kipper pâté is that most loved of British – let's face it – fish pastes. The less seen bloater paste, made from herrings, smoked whole and complete with guts intact, is most definitely on a par with a good kipper 'paste' (the chef Jeremy Lee, incidentally, makes a fine one at his restaurant Quo Vadis), although the bloater itself is more difficult to find, these days. (Go to the Butley Oysterage smokehouse in the seaside village of Orford, Suffolk, if you wish to buy some of the best bloaters I've ever tasted.) By the way, I see absolutely no reason at all not to use those rather sweet kipper fillets in vacuum packets for this pâté, complete with that dinky little flower-shaped disk of butter showing through the packaging. Ha! – a rare moment of ease, here, from your exacting cookery writer.

A fine, well-made braise is something I both love cooking and, of course, eventually eating. And, you know, I think many who cook for a living sometimes forget this most obvious of culinary journeys. However startling a plate of food may look (I am thinking competitive TV programmes, here), together with all that that implies, it occasionally occurs to me that the very idea of how it will eventually taste has, in fact, not been wholly considered by the cook in question. And, furthermore, would there actually be enough time to make a braise during one of these shows?

And there lies the rub. There is, quite simply, not enough time to cook something such as the braise featured on the menu given here: lamb shanks and white beans. Apart from anything else, what on earth would the contestant do with the time spent waiting for it to cook? I mean, one couldn't have the viewer observe a competitor twiddling their thumbs. Surely not. But – and this is a *big* but – the very idea that aspirational cooking should ever be seen as 'competitive' negates the whole ethos of intention: quite simply, to cook something rather nice and then enjoy eating it. This is not rocket science.

A perfect and proper pavlova is not simply a baked meringue. Moreover, it is something that more resembles – and tastes like – a soft marshmallow cake. This is due to two very important ingredients apart from whipped egg whites and sugar: an added modicum of both vinegar and cornflour. These two elements beaten into the mixture are what produces the unique texture of a pavlova, once cooked. There *is* a finished crust to the cake, but a softer and more yielding one than that of the crunch and shatter of a plain meringue case. Whatever you may ever have read to the contrary, please ignore. Finally, don't overdo the fruit decoration. In this case, passion fruit which, for me, is as perfect a finish as you could wish for – and rather pretty, too, if I may say.

Margarita

MAKES 4

ice cubes
200ml tequila
125ml Cointreau
80ml lime juice
fine salt
a small wedge of lime

Firstly, place four Margarita glasses in the freezer. Fill a large cocktail shaker (or jug) with lots of ice and add the alcohols and lime juice. Vigorously shake (or stir). Fill a saucer with a thick layer of salt, take the lime wedge and tweak it, then rub around the rims of the glasses. Dip the rims in the salt, shake off any excess and then strain the Margarita between the four glasses. Repeat, if in a very party mood...

Guacamole with tortilla chips

SERVES 4

2 large, ripe Hass avocados, skins and stone removed, then coarsely chopped
juice of 2 limes
2–3 jalapeño chillies, if possible, finely chopped
(use mild green chillies if jalapeños are not available)
2 tbsp finely chopped coriander leaves
4 spring onions, trimmed of most of the green parts, finely chopped
salt
plain tortilla chips

To make the guacamole, mix the first five ingredients together in a bowl. Season with salt to taste, then press a sheet of clingfilm over the surface and put in the fridge to chill until ready to decant into a pretty dish. Hand the tortilla chips alongside.

Cucumber salad

SERVES 4

2 cucumbers, peeled
1 level tbsp Maldon sea salt
1 tbsp smooth Dijon mustard
1 dsp red wine vinegar
4 tbsp sunflower oil
2 tbsp olive oil
a trickle of hot water
1 level tbsp snipped chives
freshly ground white pepper

Cut the cucumbers in half lengthways and scoop out the seeds with a teaspoon. Now, thinly slice the cucumber halves, spread them out on to a work surface and sprinkle evenly with the sea salt. Mess them around a bit with your hands until the salt has been well distributed, pile them into a colander and set over a bowl to allow excess liquid to leech out. Allow about 30–40 minutes for this, then tip out on to a tea towel and pat dry.

·

To make the dressing, put the mustard, vinegar and some pepper into a roomy bowl and whisk together. Mix both the oils together in a jug and, continuing to whisk, slowly incorporate them into the mustard mixture. As it begins to thicken, add a touch of hot water to loosen the dressing then continue to add a touch more oil. Once it is of a coating consistency and the taste is harmonious (it should be a touch sharp – at least for me, it should), tip in the cucumber and chives then gently, but thoroughly, mix together. Place in the fridge for 30 minutes until cool. Divide the salad between four pretty plates and serve at once.

Kipper pâté

SERVES 4

2 x 200g packets of kipper fillets
200g unsalted melted butter
125g cream cheese
juice of 1 lemon
Tabasco sauce
salt, if necessary

Poach the packets of kipper fillets in a pan of simmering water, cooking them for about half the time suggested on the packet. Lift out and leave to cool for 5 minutes. Snip the packets open with a pair of scissors and slide on to a deep plate or tray. Scrape away all skin, remove the minimal central cartilage and flake the cleaned flesh into the bowl of a food processor.

Now suspend a small sieve over the processor bowl and pour all the buttery packet juices, skin and bits into the sieve. Compress this debris with the back of a ladle so that every scrap of kipper essence is forced through it. Pulse the mixture for a few seconds, but only to break it up. Add 150g of the melted butter, the cream cheese, lemon juice and a few drops of Tabasco, to taste, then process to a smooth purée and check for seasoning. Spoon into small pots, smooth over the surface of each and seal with the remaining 50g melted butter. Put the pots to chill in the fridge for at least a couple of hours. Eat with hot toast. (Once sealed, the pâté will keep, chilled, for 4–5 days.)

Braised lamb shanks with white beans

SERVES 4

350g dried white beans

400g cherry tomatoes

8 cloves of garlic

several sprigs of thyme, leaves stripped off by hand

200ml sweet vermouth

2 tbsp olive oil

250g fatty, unsmoked streaky bacon, in a piece, rind removed and cut into 2cm chunks

4 lamb shanks, approx. 1.7kg total weight

300g onions, chopped

300g carrots, peeled and chopped into small chunks

2 bay leaves

5 cloves

350ml tasty stock (beef, chicken, vegetable or, best of all, lamb!)

3 tbsp finely chopped parsley

salt and pepper

Put the beans in a roomy pan and cover with water (no salt) to at least 4cm above the beans. Bring up to a boil, switch off the heat and leave in the water for 1 hour – or longer, if desired, as they won't spoil.

Put the tomatoes in a liquidiser together with the garlic (unpeeled), thyme leaves and vermouth and process until smooth. Suspend a fine sieve over a deep pan or bowl and tip the mixture into it. Press well down into the sieve with a small ladle until a 'raw tomato soup' has been passed through from the messy mulch (skins, seeds, etc.), which should then be discarded. Now put this mixture to one side.

Using a large, preferably cast-iron pot (a Le Creuset would be ideal) heat the olive oil over a moderate flame. Tip in the bacon and allow to fry quietly for about 5 minutes, or until lightly gilded and its fat has run. Lift out the bacon and reserve on a large plate. Season the shanks and slowly fry in the bacon fat until all surfaces are nicely browned. Lift out and place alongside the bacon. Now introduce the onions and carrots to the pot and allow them to sweat for about 10 minutes, or until lightly coloured. Add the tomato mixture, bring up to a bubble and allow to cook for a further 10 minutes. Stir in the bay leaves, cloves and stock. Now, reintroduce the bacon and lamb shanks and push under the liquid to cover them. Bring up to a simmer, partially cover the pot and cook very slowly, for 1 hour.

Preheat the oven to 150°C/gas mark 2. By this time the beans should have had their hour's soak. Drain them, rinse well and return them to the pot in

which they soaked. Cover with fresh water and bring them up to a simmer (again, no salt). Allow to cook quietly for about 20 minutes, switch off the heat, cover and put to one side.

•

Once the lamb has had its hour's simmering, drain the beans once more and stir into the partly stewed lamb and vegetables. Stir together well, thoroughly distributing the beans among the meat. Bring up to a quiet but significant simmer before sliding into the oven. Cook for a further 1½ hours, uncovered, until both beans and lamb are meltingly tender and the liquid surrounding them has somewhat reduced, having by now formed a nice and gooey burnished look to the surface of the stew. Remove from the oven, add the parsley and carefully stir it in. Serve just as it is, directly from the pot, into heated plates, at table.

Pavlova

a little softened butter
4 large egg whites
pinch of salt
250g caster sugar, plus extra for the cake tin and the top of the cake
2 heaped tsp cornflour
1 dsp cider vinegar
1 tsp vanilla extract
300ml double cream
1 tbsp caster sugar
about 12 passion fruit, as wizened as possible, as these will give the most perfumed seeds

Preheat the oven to 150°C/gas mark 2.

Line the base of a deep, loose-bottomed and, preferably, non-stick cake tin (at least 20 x 5cm) with a circle of dampened greaseproof paper. Generously butter the sides of the tin, then generously dust them with caster sugar, shaking off any excess.

Using an electric mixer (or sturdy electric hand-whisk) whisk the egg whites, together with the salt, to soft peaks. With the motor still running, introduce the caster sugar in heaped tablespoonfuls, until the meringue is stiff and satin-like. Now, quickly and thoroughly beat in the cornflour, vinegar and vanilla extract.

Carefully pile into the cake tin and smooth over the surface with a dampened spatula. Strew the surface with a light dusting of caster sugar and then bake in the oven for about 1 hour – or as long as 1¼ hours – until the pavlova has risen somewhat, developed a pale golden crust and is springy when prodded with a finger. Now close the oven door and switch off the heat, leaving the pavlova until completely cold; this is most important, so ensuring that the pavlova sinks as little as possible. Once cool, run a small, sharp knife around the inside of the tin, unmould the pavlova then turn it out on to a presentable plate and peel off the circle of greaseproof paper.

Whip together the cream and 1 tablespoon of sugar until loosely thick, then pile over the surface of the pavlova with the same spatula, making seductive swirls. Finally, strew the passion fruit pulp willy-nilly all over the cream, even allowing some of it to dribble down the sides of the pavlova. Cut into nice big wedges and eat with abandon.

Conversion chart
·
Acknowledgements
·
Index

Conversion chart

Weight

15g	½oz	500g	1lb 2oz
20g	¾oz	550g	1¼lb
25g	1oz	600g	1lb 5oz
40g	1½oz	650g	1lb 7oz
50g	2oz	700g	1½lb
65g	2½oz	750g	1lb 10oz
75g	3oz	800g	1lb 12oz
90g	3½oz	850g	1lb 14oz
110g	4oz	900g	2lb
125g	4½oz	950g	2lb 2oz
150g	5oz	1kg	2¼lb
175g	6oz	1.4kg	3lb
200g	7oz	1.5kg	3lb 5oz
225g	8oz (½lb)	1.6kg	3½lb
250g	9oz	1.7kg	3¾lb
275g	10oz	1.8kg	4lb
310g	11oz	2kg	4½lb
350g	12oz	2.3kg	5lb
375g	13oz	2.5kg	5½lb
400g	14oz	2.7kg	6lb
450g	1lb	3kg	6½lb

Volume

Metric	Imperial		
25ml	1fl oz	1 litre	1¾ pints
50ml	2fl oz	1.1 litres	2 pints
75ml	3fl oz	1.25 litres	2¼ pints
90ml	3½fl oz	1.4 litres	2½ pints
100ml	4fl oz	1.6 litres	2¾ pints
125ml	4½fl oz	1.75 litres	3 pints
150ml	5fl oz (¼ pint)	1.8 litres	3¼ pints
175ml	6fl oz	2 litres	3½ pints
200ml	7fl oz	2.1 litres	3¾ pints
225ml	8fl oz	2.3 litres	4 pints
250ml	9fl oz	2.75 litres	4¾ pints
300ml	10fl oz (½ pint)	3.4 litres	6 pints
350ml	12fl oz	3.9 litres	7 pints
400ml	14fl oz	4.5 litres	8 pints (1 gallon)
450ml	¾ pint		
500ml	18fl oz		
600ml	1 pint	teaspoon (tsp) = 5ml	
750ml	1¼ pints	dessert spoon (dsp) = 10ml	
900ml	1½ pints	tablespoon (tbsp) = 15ml	

Oven temperatures

140°C	Fan 120°C	275°F	Gas Mark 1
150°C	Fan 130°C	300°F	Gas Mark 2
160°C	Fan 140°C	325°F	Gas Mark 3
180°C	Fan 160°C	350°F	Gas Mark 4
190°C	Fan 170°C	375°F	Gas Mark 5
200°C	Fan 180°C	400°F	Gas Mark 6
220°C	Fan 200°C	425°F	Gas Mark 7
230°C	Fan 210°C	450°F	Gas Mark 8
240°C	Fan 220°C	475°F	Gas Mark 9

Index

A

after-show supper *see* supper, after-show
ajo blanco 60, 64–5
Allard, Madame 244
almond
    ajo blanco 65
    & raspberry baked soufflé puddings 96–7
    spiced 210, 213
anchovy
    Jansson's Temptation 211, 218–19
    rosemary, garlic & roast leg of lamb 37, 48–9
    on toast 18, 20–1
Angostura bitters
    champagne cocktail 80–1
    Gibson 190, 192
    with orange & pink grapefruit salad 227, 238–9
apple sauce 79, 95
artichoke, globe, with mustard vinaigrette 36, 42–3
asparagus with sauce mousseline 171, 180–1
aubergine with ginger, spring onion & red chilli 60–1, 66–7
avocado
    cream, with sea bass, marinated with lime, chilli & coriander 190, 194–5
    guacamole with tortilla chips 246–7

B

bacon
    Bacon du Bedat 210, 216–17
    braised lamb shanks with white beans 252–5
    tarte flambée 174–6
Bareham, Lindsey 36–7
basil ice cream 127, 142–3
bean
    green, salad, with shallots & cream 18, 22–3
    white, with braised lamb shanks 245, 252–5
béarnaise sauce, with grilled fillet steak 103, 108–10
beef
    consommé, Bullshot 226, 228–9
    grilled fillet steak with béarnaise sauce 103, 108–10
    mince, horseradish cream with beetroot jelly 84–7
    tea, cup of, with Madeira 210, 214–15
beetroot
    English salad 149, 156–7
    jelly, with fresh horseradish cream 78, 84–7
Bentley, Vanessa 191, 202–4
biscuits, Lancashire cheese & onion 148, 152–3
Bloody Mary 126, 128–9
bread
    & butter pudding, hot cross bun 171, 184–5

---

    big fried, veal kidney on 227, 236–7
    tiny fennel-salami sandwiches 36, 40–1
    see also toast
breakfast, a substantial late weekend 223–39
    baked mushrooms with tomatoes 226, 230–3
    Bullshot 226, 228–9
    devils on horseback 226, 228–9
    kedgeree 227, 234–5
    orange & pink grapefruit salad with Angostura bitters 227, 238–9
    veal kidney on big fried bread 227, 236–7
brown shrimp
    dill & leeks, warm salad of 126–7, 134–5
    potted 170–1, 178–9
Brussels sprout, buttered 79, 94
Bullshot 226, 228–9

C

cake, sponge 52–5
Campari, negroni 21
candied orange peel 103, 120–1
caramel custard, coffee 30–1
carrot
    & peas, stewed 149, 162–3
    braised lamb shanks with white beans 252–5
    peas & chicken pie 149, 158–61
celebratory dinner *see* dinner, celebratory
celeriac, cream of celery soup 155
celery
    cream of, soup 148–9, 154–5
    nibbles 126, 128–9
champagne
    cocktail 78, 80–1
    French 75 210, 212
    Mimosa 170, 172–3
cheese
    gougères 78, 82–3
    Lancashire, & onion biscuits 148, 152–3
    see also cream cheese; Parmesan
chicken
    paella 26–8
    pie, with peas & carrots 149, 158–61
chickpea, hummus 63
chips 103, 112
chorizo sausage, paella 26–8
cocktail, champagne 78, 80–1
cod's roe, smoked, on toast with devilled eggs 78–9, 88–9
coffee caramel custard 19, 30–1
Cognac, champagne cocktail 80–1
Cointreau
    margarita 246–7
    Mimosa 170, 172–3
    The Unknown Soldier 103, 118–19
Conran, Sir Terence 148–9